My Mother's Daughter

A Heritage of Faith, Service, Wisdom, and Love

My Mother's Daughter

A Heritage of Faith, Service, Wisdom, and Love

An Anthology
Curated and Edited by

Paulette Norvel Lewis

My Mother's Daughter: A Heritage of Faith, Service, Wisdom, and Love

Text copyright © 2024 by Paulette Norvel Lewis

Email inquiries to Paulette Norvel Lewis at paulette20133@gmail.com

ISBN 979-8-9906589-0-5 (Hard Cover)
ISBN 979-8-9906589-2-9 (Paperback)
ISBN 979-8-9906589-1-2 (eBook)

Cover design by Donald Bermudez, Studio Named Bermudez

Cover photo by Harding Norvell

Editing by Paulette Norvel Lewis and Bonnie B. Daneker

Interior design and formatting by Becky's Graphic Design®, LLC

Dedication

This book is dedicated to my beautiful mother, Velma Hadessa Wilson Norvel, and all Black mothers, especially those represented in this book as well as to my beautiful sisters, Kirticina Norvel Twine and Carolyn Norvel who, with my mother, grace the cover of this book. All of you have sacrificed and worked tirelessly throughout the years to provide safety, sustenance, shelter, guidance, a faith foundation, and a good example for your children and those you love. You endowed us with a precious heritage of FAITH, COURAGE, SERVICE, WISDOM, and LOVE. And, all the while, you remembered and honored who YOU were.

Please know that . . .

We "SEE" you! We BLESS you! We THANK you, and we will always LOVE YOU!

Introduction

After making a Women's Day announcement at a Sunday church service, Mrs. Geraldine Barker approached me and said: "I don't know your mother, but I see her in everything that you do." I was too stunned to ask her what she meant but I knew the comment was meant to be a compliment so, it stuck with me. Growing up, I was always told that I looked like my father and my grandmother, and that is true. However, after thinking about that "out-of-the-blue" comment a bit more, its meaning clearly explained why, as I have gotten older, I am sometimes told that I look like my mother. My demeanor, gestures, and how I approach things, are indeed, like my mother and I am sometimes shocked when I see her in my mirror. Mrs. Barker accurately perceived that "I Am My Mother's Daughter." As we say in the Black community, "I am marked!"

My mother was wise and beautiful, and I am honored to be compared to her in any way. I only wish that I had inherited her warm hazel eyes and her infectious laughter.

I have many friends and family members who had/have close relationships with their mothers and who frequently quote their mothers' wisdom and counsel. I was fortunate enough to share in some of these remarkable relationships first-hand. I remember when the mother of my friend, Beverly Beavers-Brooks (formerly Lyle) died. Beverly and her mother lived in different cities however, they talked on the phone daily. As soon as her close friends heard the news of Ms. Ophelia's death, we hurried to Beverly's side to comfort her. Inevitably, we began telling stories about her mother. At one point, we were all crying. Beverly stopped suddenly and reminded us that it was HER mother who had passed away. We all burst into laughter.

We often hear about the special relationships that Black men have with their mothers and we see it frequently displayed as big burly football players send greetings and love to their mothers and grandmothers in the middle of intense Sunday competitions. On the other hand, we seldom hear about the special relationships that I know Black women also have with their mothers and grandmothers. I frequently hear my friends refer to their mothers as "strong," "graceful," "determined," "sassy," "faith-FULL," "visionary," "loving," "wise," and "generous, among other things."

They are our role models, best friends, confidants, cheerleaders, and sheroes. I hear stories (especially at funerals) about how they fed the hungry, cared for the sick and elderly, visited the imprisoned, clothed the naked, fought for justice, loved, advocated for children, spoke truth to power, welcomed strangers, dressed "to kill," and were great cooks.

I know that I am attracted to my friends and maintain close relationships with them because they have similar values, are women of integrity, people of God, and use their strengths and talents to help build the Kingdom of God. I often wonder about the legacies we will leave that are rooted in the examples of our wonderful mothers. I am curious about the lessons we all learned from our mothers that are now, whether consciously or unconsciously, perpetuated in us and passed on to our children, grandchildren, step-children, "adopted" children, and godchildren.

Through their stories and photos, I have tried to capture the legacies of faith, service, wisdom, and love endowed to us by our mothers. I know that many of you will recognize some of these traits in your mothers and yourselves. I hope that you will be inspired and encouraged by the strong Black women, the unsung sheroes, represented herein and I hope that you will share their immortal messages, and yours, with future generations.

I am deeply grateful to each woman (family and friends) who contributed to this anthology. I hope that you will treasure and regard your story as a special tribute to your beloved mothers. I certainly do.

As I was writing this foreword while visiting a dear friend, Jackie James (who did not know what I was doing) spontaneously remarked: "You are so much like your mother." When I asked what she meant she responded that how I do things, and my "ways" were like my mother's. "She was very precise and did things very carefully and caringly." This was the second time that I had heard this comment from someone and, this time, I did not doubt that it was a compliment. I am my mother's daughter.

Acknowledgments

I am eternally grateful to Mrs. Gloria Broadus Caponis who so generously opened her home and provided surrogate parenting for me (a stranger!) so that I could attend a "Black" Catholic high school nearly fifty miles from my home. (That's another story!) As a master teacher, she knew the importance of education and she knew its importance to my parents and me. She clearly understood that "it takes a village." Her selflessness and generosity were invaluable gifts that changed the trajectory of my life and continue to enrich it. Without the education that she made possible for me; this book would not exist.

I am grateful to my husband, Marion for his support, encouragement, and patience during my laborious but inspiring task of curating and editing this anthology. With his encouragement and that of my dear "sister," Alexis, I was able to move from a place of fear to empowerment. Alexis' expertise, experience, and commitment to the success of my project were invaluable in helping me to move the book from concept to actualization to market. I am so grateful that she pushed and pulled until she was sure I understood the process.

Thanks to Faith Cola for her support. I can always count on her to help with my many projects. I am very grateful to Melvia Wallace for lending her professional editing skills and for her support and attention to detail in helping me to bring clarity to some of the ideas in the various essays. Donald Bermudez provided invaluable design assistance. I greatly appreciate his contribution, encouragement, and support.

I am especially grateful to the women who trusted me and took the time to write these moving testimonials of love and devotion in honor of their mothers. I appreciate their patience as I continued to email for more details and photos. Most of all, I thank their mothers and mine for their love and for being the light unto our paths and futures. They will forever be in our hearts.

Finally, thank you, Mrs. Barker, mother of six! Without your comment, this book would not have been inspired or completed.

May God bless all of you "real good."

Highlights

"My mother believed in education like the devil believes sin!"
—*Dr. Johnnetta Betsch Cole*

"Mom, you must have heard them. They called me a nigger!" She calmly corrected me and said, "No, they did not . . . I want you to always remember this: they did not call you a nigger because that is not who you are! You can never, ever, let anybody else define who you are. You must always define for yourself who you are!"
—*The Honorable Glenda Hatchett*

". . . at my mother's funeral when a former student, now a high school principal, gave his personal testimony about her. At age fourteen, he could not read. My mother asked him what he wanted to do more than anything else in life. He said he wanted to learn to drive a car. My mother drove him to the Mobile Driver License Office where, together, they picked up all the driving manuals. Using the manuals, she proceeded to teach him to read so that he could pass the driver's license exam and achieve his dream. She always said, 'There is no such thing as a dumb child. Only a child you havn't found a way to reach.'"
—*The Honorable Alexis Herman*

"Growing up, it was an unspoken expectation that all four of my parents' children would attend college. While we had the freedom to choose where we would go, we did not have the choice not to go."
—*Dr. Melvia L. Wallace*

"My mother's deep interest in the life and history of African Americans led our family to move to Tuskegee, AL, where she led the Red Cross, and my surgeon father led the NAACP."
—*The Honorable Constance Newman*

"Mama got on her knees right there in the bank and prayed fervently to the Lord."
—*Letetia Daniels Jackson*

Contents

"I have great faith in the power of women
who will dedicate themselves wholeheartedly
to the task of remaking our society."

Mrs. Coretta Scott King

Clemmie Barnes Hatchett, Ed.D.
(Photo courtesy of Glenda Hatchett, Esq.)

"My mother was a badass Black woman, and I say that with the highest degree of respect!"

— Glenda Hatchett, Esq.

HONORING

Clemmie Elizabeth Barnes Hatchett, Ed.D.

Written by Glenda Hatchett, Esq. / Daughter

I have never known, nor will I ever know anyone remotely like my mother. Smart, bold, strong, resourceful, savvy, sassy, beautiful, tenacious, creative, resilient, clever, extremely generous, bossy, feisty, fearless: that was my mother. Above all else, however, she was a woman deeply rooted in her faith and unapologetically her authentic self.

Clemmie Elizabeth Barnes Hatchett was one of my grandparents' nine children and the youngest of their six daughters. She and her family were poor by monetary standards but wealthy beyond measure in love and faith: a kind of wealth that no amount of money could ever buy. Despite growing up poor and Black, in the grips of the insidious ramifications of segregation in the deep South, where racism and sexism were enforced obstructions, she graduated as valedictorian of her class and dared to dream of being a pediatrician. I am certain she would have gone on to become the U.S. Surgeon General had she been afforded a fraction of the opportunities afforded to me. My mother was a *BADASS* Black woman, and I say that with the highest degree of respect!

My mother dedicated her professional life to public education. Her commitment to her students was indeed her ministry. I have a vivid and special memory of an encounter I had on my way to an event on the campus of Yale University. I was approached by a student who learned that my last name was Hatchett. He asked if Mrs. Hatchett was my mother. I responded with a smile, "Yes, she is." With emotion in his voice, he told me: "I would not be a senior at Yale University if your mother had not been my elementary school teacher!" He added, "She believed in me when people didn't believe a boy from 'Buttermilk Bottom' could be somebody." He went on for a long time telling me what my mother meant to him and how she cared for so many children. I was always very proud of her but at that moment, I was bursting with pride! Later in life, Mom went on to get her master's degree in early childhood education and a doctorate in educational administration.

My mother was a perfectionist. I am not. Even though she was my most severe critic, she was also my most zealous advocate, defender, and supporter. She demanded the best of me and, at times, saw far more in me than I saw in myself. Mom often challenged me to stretch further than I thought I could reach. She not only believed in dreaming bold dreams but also in being intentional about using one's marvelous gifts to benefit others.

Mom's philosophy, which I have adopted and truly strive to live by, is that you must "lift as you climb." She instilled in me the idea that your blessings are not for you to hoard, but rather, they are given to you so that you may bless others.

My mother, a beaming light of a woman, had an unquenchable thirst for life and adventure. Her ardor and intention for living were magnificent, and she remained curious even in her last years. She disregarded limitations and took "reaching for the sky" quite literally. Mom took pilot lessons at ninety years of age with the intent of flying coast to coast! She drove her hard-top convertible sports car until she was ninety-seven: hood retracted, dark glasses on, the wind blowing through her hair, at speeds beyond the limit!

We did all kinds of things together. Whether we were in her kitchen or exploring the coral reefs in Australia, the quality time that I spent with my mother was some of the best times of my life! She loved traveling extensively throughout the world so, some of the most memorable times are of the two of us traveling to various places abroad. One of my favorite memories is of the time Mom insisted that we go into a casino in Cairo, Egypt. When we entered, a very telling hush fell over the small, dimly lit room filled with men (very wealthy Arabic men, I might add). I said, "Mom, there are no women in here. Let's go." She immediately responded, "Yes, there are. We are here." And then, with the most confident strut, she made her way to the Blackjack table and gracefully took a seat. Given her physical appearance, they probably assumed that she was a wealthy Arabic woman and that I was her handmaid. Once seated, we learned that the minimum bid was $5,000! So, I knew that we would be leaving immediately . . . or so I thought! Instead, my fabulously dramatic mother reached for her purse. I was hyperventilating at this point because I thought she was about to pull out her American Express card, and I knew I would never be able to explain this to Daddy when we returned home. In a performance that could have won her an Academy Award, Mom calmly declared, "Oh my goodness, I left my source of funds upstairs. I'll be back shortly." She looked at me, stood, and with that same confident strut, walked out with me trailing behind. We laughed about that for years! This casino adventure is a small, yet very graphic example of who my mother was—a fearless spirit.

Mom always said she would live to be at least 120 years old. God called her home a few months before her ninety-ninth birthday. She was not denied, however. She miraculously packed 120 years of living and loving into ninety-eight years. Her love of life was infectious! Her life itself was her gift to everyone who loved her.

In closing, I want to share one of many essential life lessons that Mom taught me when I was about nine years old. As we left a store in Atlanta's West End and began walking to our car, two white boys glared at me and shouted, "Nigger!" I was upset, and I expected my mother to do something. I asked her, "Mom, did you hear what they called me?" She instructed me to get in the car. I was very confused so I continued to press her, "Mom, you must have heard them. They called me a nigger!" She calmly corrected me and said, "No, they did not." By then, I was distraught and confused. I thought to myself, "*Clearly, she heard them. Why doesn't she do something?!*" Disappointed, I again said, "Mom, you had to have heard them." She turned to me and said, "I want you to always remember this; they did not call you a nigger because that is not who you are! You can never, ever, let anybody else define who you are. You must always define for yourself who you are!" I didn't fully understand or appreciate the life lesson then, but Lord knows, I have reflected on that day many times, and I'm thankful for that lesson. Through my life's journey, I have never EVER allowed anyone else to define who I am, and I never will.

I will be forever grateful for the gift of Clemmie Elizabeth Barnes Hatchett. And I am immensely thankful for a mother who challenged me to be the best version of myself. I thank God for all the magnificent moments we shared and the memories that make me feel extremely blessed to be her daughter.

The Honorable Glenda Hatchett, Esq.
Atlanta, GA

Judge Glenda Hatchett
(Photo courtesy of Glenda Hatchett)

The Honorable Glenda Hatchett is a prominent American television personality, attorney, author, judge, and star of the Emmy-awarded courtroom show, *Judge Hatchett* and *The Verdict with Judge Hatchett* for the past twenty-three years. She is also currently practicing law at Stewart Miller Simmons Trial Attorneys in Atlanta.

After completing college, Judge Hatchett served as a clerk at the U.S. District Court in the Northern District of Georgia. She later worked at Delta Airlines as Senior Attorney and Public Relations Manager becoming the company's highest-ranking woman of color worldwide. As Senior Attorney, she represented the company in labor and anti-trust cases and participated in merger negotiations. She was later promoted to manager of Delta's public relations department, handling global crisis management and media relations for the U.S., Europe, and Asia.

Upon her appointment to the Fulton County Juvenile Court in 1991, Hatchett became the first African American Chief Judge of the State of Georgia. In collaboration with the Atlanta Bar Association and Alston & Bird, Hatchett helped found the Truancy Intervention Project, an early intervention program for truant children.

In 1998, Hatchett resigned from the Fulton County Juvenile Court to spend time with her two children before accepting an offer from Sony Pictures Television to have her own television show, *Judge Hatchett*. While filming *Judge Hatchett, she* released her first self-help book, *Say What You Mean and Mean What You Say!: Saving Your Child from a Troubled World*. She released her second book, *Dare to Take Charge: How to Live Your Life on Purpose*, in 2012.

In 2014, Hatchett established The Hatchett Firm, which focused on wrongful death, catastrophic injury, medical malpractice, product liability, class action, premises liability, and social security cases. Concerned about police brutality against African American men, Hatchett announced that she would represent Philando Castile's family in 2016.

Judge Hatchett has used her considerable influence to raise awareness about critical issues such as parental responsibility, the well-being of children, and police violence against Black males. Like her mother, she is a compassionate and passionate advocate for children and works with the National CARES for Mentoring Movement to provide support and guidance for vulnerable children.

In addition to her civic contributions, Hatchett has received numerous awards, including the Roscoe Pound Award, the National Council on Crime and Delinquency's highest recognition, and the NAACP Thurgood Marshall Award. The Girl Scouts of the United States of America named Hatchett one of its Ten National Women of Distinction. She has served on multiple boards, including the National Football League's Atlanta Falcons' Board of Advisors. She is featured in *TheHistoryMakers*.

Judge Hatchett graduated from Mount Holyoke College with a degree in political science and from Emory University School of Law. She is the proud mother of two sons and grandmother of two grandsons.

Mrs. Leteria Seals Clemons

(Photo by Michael Alexander, courtesy of Paulette Lewis)

"At age fifty, I have come to cherish my mom, the original influencer, for being at the cutting edge of all things, and for challenging me to do the same."

— Lybra Clemons

HONORING

Mrs. Leteria Seals Clemons

Written by Lybra Clemons / Daughter

Mothers and daughters can be tricky. As daughters, our mothers are our first role models, and we spend our early years learning and mimicking their habits, their walk, their talk, their likes, their demeanor, and oftentimes, their styles. Then comes that moment when we realize that we want to be our own person. So, while we have spent our formative years learning and mimicking, we spend our adolescent years trying to subconsciously undo and defy it, while still craving the gaze and connection to our mothers.

And then at that pivotal moment in our lives, the onset of adulthood, we find ourselves wanting all the best of our moms to show up in everything that you do. We walk by a mirror, and we catch glimpses of our moms and realize that it pleases us more than it displeases us. The way we talk, the way we communicate, and the way that we engage with other women becomes more aligned with how we see our moms as a human rather than as a mom. And that is likely one of the most precious gifts that one will ever receive. Nevertheless, the ebbs and flows of mother-daughter relationships remain tricky.

I love my mom. Although everyone compares me to my dad, I see so much of who I am in my mom. I was that teenager who just wanted my own space (space meaning, I wanted not to be my mom). Not because I didn't love or adore her, but because, as a child, I didn't want to explore my life in the shadow of such a great influencer. You see, my mom was and still is, an influencer. These days, people refer to "influencers" as larger-than-life celebrities who have amassed a great deal of social media followers. Those "influencers" (i.e. the Kardashians) set the rules, endorse products, and influence an entire generation on the latest fashion, music, entertainment, and social commentary. They are trendsetters.

My mom, however, was an influencer in other ways. She influenced me in ways that I once found to be incredibly overwhelming, but now have come to cherish because, it is because of her, that I AM. My mom, the influencer, always had a point of view, she knew how and when to run a household, how to manage tough situations, how to navigate social constructs, how to present herself with confidence without arrogance, how to subtly make a point using diplomacy, and do it in the most loving and giving way that any person ever could. It's the Leteria Clemons "flair" that sets her apart, and it just seems so effortless. While I have seen so many people and women do the expected, my mom has always wanted to do the unexpected. She has influenced so many people around her because of her demeanor, approach, and attitude. It wasn't until I started writing this that I realized how many people are in awe of my mom, in a way that I wasn't until recently.

Lybra Clemons and her sister, Lailee Clemons
(Photo courtesy of Lybra Clemons)

What some people close to her know, but many don't, is that my mom LOVES harder than any person I know. Her love for me, my sister, and my dad is beyond comprehension. We all have various definitions of love, but anyone who knows my mom would agree that she loves her family using every definition of the word. She loves so hard sometimes that it comes at her own expense. But that is a chance that she is always willing to take.

Lybra and her mom, Mrs. Leteria Clemons
(Photo courtesy of Lybra Clemons)

At age fifty, I have come to cherish my mom, the original influencer, for being at the cutting edge of all things; and for challenging me to do the same. But more importantly, I cherish her for being the person who influenced me to be who I am today. Change agents are not a dime a dozen, and embracing and promoting innovative ideas and thought leadership is not for everyone. But it is for me. My career and entire life have been built on being the first, a change agent, a thought leader, and a creative. Why? Because that is my mom. I learned her ways and have embraced them as honestly and diplomatically as I know how.

So, when people say, "I see so much of your mom in you," I don't automatically think about my nose, eyes, hands, or physical traits that remind them of her; I think of the characteristics of a humble warrior. That is what I believe they see in me. And that is the very essence of my mom.

Lybra Clemons
Sarasota, FL

Lybra Clemons
(Photo courtesy of Lybra Clemons)

Lybra S. Clemons is recognized as a Diversity and Inclusion (DEI) "Trailblazer." She is a seasoned C-suite executive with twenty years of Human Resources, Talent, Culture, and DEI experience across Fortune 500 companies globally, including Twillio, Inc. PayPal, Morgan Stanley, and American Express. She has created, built, and implemented practical strategies that result in stronger retention of top talent and higher engagement of the workforce from the frontline worker to the C-suite. Lybra has advised CEOs, led and scaled talent and diversity teams, managed mergers and acquisitions cultural integrations, developed a strategy for managing hybrid and distributed workforce efforts, contributed to ESG data and reporting, and drove projects specific to company transformations.

Lybra, recently joined EQ, a transformative and inclusive AI talent acquisition tool, as an EQbuddy. Advisor. She believes that this tool is exactly what has been missing in helping to effectively identify stellar global talent at all levels.

Ms. Clemons has a B.A. from Spelman College in political science, a master's degree in public administration from Columbia University School of Public Administration and International Affairs and has completed the Executive Management Program at The Tucks School of Business at Dartmouth. She is a Trustee at the American Folk Art Museum and a member of Black Women on Boards. She has a Cyber Risk and Strategy Certification from Diligent and Black Corporate Board Readiness from Santa Clara University Leavey School of Business.

Vonnetta Epps and mom, Benita Epps

(Photo by Rahaad Little, courtesy of Vonnetta Epps)

"We have participated in various events together: parades, and community service activities, working side by side to make a positive impact on our community."

— Vonnetta Epps

HONORING

Mrs. Benita Lewis Epps

Written by Vonnetta Epps / Daughter

In the fabric of my life, my mother stands as my hero, playing numerous roles that have shaped me into the person I am today. She is my best friend and nurturing caregiver, an inspiring teacher, and so much more. Her impact on my life is immeasurable. In this essay, I want to share the profound influence my mother has had on me and how her love, support, and guidance have shaped my values, aspirations, and the way I navigate the world.

Mrs. Benita Epps

(Photo courtesy of Vonnetta Epps)

My Best Friend and Prayer Warrior: A pillar of support, my mother has been more than just a parent; she has been my confidante, my rock, and my best friend. She has stood by my side through every decision I have made, offering sage guidance and encouragement. Even when I made the daunting decision to leave my lifelong home and move to a new state to change my career, her unwavering support and encouragement were the driving force behind my leap of faith. Her prayers have been a source of strength during the toughest times, reminding me that I am never alone in this journey called life.

A Nurturing Caregiver: My mother's love is beyond measure, and it has been a constant throughout my life. As my caregiver, she has tended to my physical and emotional needs with untiring dedication. I vividly remember that during the COVID-19 pandemic, she went above and beyond, caring for me while she also battled the virus. Her selflessness and dedication to my well-being are a testament to her love and commitment as a mother.

Vonnetta and her mother, Mrs. Benita Epps
(Photo courtesy of Vonnetta Epps)

Teacher and Mentor: Beyond being my mother, she also served as my 7th-grade math teacher. Her excellence in education extended beyond the classroom, as she taught me valuable life lessons and shaped my character. She has empowered me to become the woman I am today, instilling in me a thirst for knowledge and a drive to constantly better myself.

A Sorority Sister and Community Leader: Growing up, I had the privilege of witnessing my mother's active involvement in our community as a member of Alpha Kappa Alpha

Sorority, Inc. Her dedication to service inspired me to follow in her footsteps. Together, we have participated in various events, parades, and community service activities, working side by side to make a positive impact on our community. Her example has taught me the importance of giving back and being a catalyst for change. As a math teacher, mentor, community leader, and woman of faith, she has made a difference not only in my life but also in the lives of countless youth in the city of LaGrange, GA.

My Travel Partner: Some of my most cherished lifelong memories and adventures are those that were created and shared with my mother. We took our first international trip to London during my senior year of high school and, we explored Mexico, Alaska, Canada, and beyond. These experiences not only broadened my horizons but also strengthened our bond. Through travel, my mother has taught me the value of embracing different cultures and perspectives and fostered a sense of curiosity and open-mindedness.

Role Model: Embodying love and respect, above all, my mother is my role model. Her grace, kindness, and genuine love for others have shaped the way I approach life. I strive to emulate her ability to carry herself with dignity and to treat everyone with respect. Her support and belief in me have given me the confidence to pursue my dreams and become the best version of myself. She not only did this for me but for my brothers and our entire family, instilling the importance of family and faith in our household.

Vonnetta and her mother, Mrs. Benita Epps
(Photo courtesy of Vonnetta Epps)

My mother's impact on my life is immeasurable. She is my best friend, an inspiring teacher, sorority sister, travel partner, and role model. She has shaped my values, aspirations, and how I navigate the world and my family. Her love, support, and guidance have given me the courage to take risks, the compassion to give back, and the strength to love fearlessly. I am forever grateful for the incredible woman she is and the profound impact she continues to have on my life.

Vonnetta LaRuth Epps
Cleveland, OH

Vonnetta LaRuth Epps
(Photo courtesy of Vonnetta Epps)

Vonnetta LaRuth Epps is a Senior Manager of Customer Solutions and Claims for Nestlé, the world's largest food and beverage company based in Cleveland, Ohio. Before joining Nestle, Vonnetta was employed by the Georgia Ports Authority in Savannah, GA for over ten years, excelling in various roles including Assistant Manager of Operations, Assistant Manager of Market Research and Development, Process Improvement Manager, and Customer Service Manager. While in Savannah, Vonnetta served on several boards including The First Tee of Savannah and Habitat for Humanity. Vonnetta established the LPGA-USGA Girls Golf of Savannah, a subsidiary program of The First Tee, and served as Site Director of that program.

A lifelong learner, Vonnetta earned an M.A. degree in Business Management and participates in Improv classes. She is an avid golfer, an active member of her sorority and church, and participates in community service opportunities. Vonnetta is an extensive traveler, and enjoys visiting family and friends. Vonnetta has a Bachelor of Arts and a Master's Degree from Savannah State University, where she received a golf scholarship.

"We as African American women
seldom do just what we want to do but,
we always do what we have to do."

Dr. Dorothy Irene Height

Mrs. Joyce Dunlap "Granny"

(Photo courtesy of Beverly Beavers-Brooks)

When I went to my mother crying, she would respond "The blacker the berry the sweeter juice. You are my sweet, beautiful little girl."

— Beverly Beavers-Brooks

HONORING

Mrs. Joyce Lipscomb Jeffrey Dunlap and Ms. Ophelia Jeffrey Beavers Daniels

Written by Beverly Beavers-Brooks / Daughter and Granddaughter

My legacy of faith, strength, resilience, and entrepreneurship begins with my grandmother, Joycie Lipscomb Jeffrey Dunlap, affectionately referred to as "Granny." Granny was the oldest of three girls. When she was twelve years old, her mother died, and she became the mother figure for her younger sisters and the primary support to her father in managing the family farm. This instilled in her a sense of responsibility, resilience, compassion, and love of family that developed her into the strong, independent matriarch that she became.

The strength Granny developed as a young girl prepared her to deal with the inevitable disappointments of life. She had a beautiful singing voice and was offered two college scholarships in music from Mary Allen College in Crockett, TX, and Tuskegee Institute in Tuskegee, AL. However, she had to decline both because of her responsibilities at home.

In 1916, Granny married my grandfather, Oscar Jeffrey, and they had five children, including my mother, Ophelia Jeffrey Beavers Daniels, the youngest child. My grandfather owned an ice delivery business; however, he died when my mother was ten years old. Granny was again in the position of having to assume tremendous responsibility as she took over the business to support her children. She drove the ice truck herself and hired male students from nearby Texas College to help deliver the ice. Always front and center in Granny's mind and heart was doing what was necessary to care for her family. As she aged, she spent quality time with each of her children and helped to raise all her grandchildren, including me and my brother, Quincy.

Granny always took her civic responsibility seriously. After Blacks were given the right to vote, she dutifully paid her poll taxes (even though it was a financial hardship), and never missed an opportunity to vote. She dutifully paid her dues to the Prince Hall Order of the Eastern Star and always adhered to its core values of faith and service. She earnestly believed that voting would make a difference in the lives of "colored" people. She cast her last vote in 1994 at the age of ninety-nine helping to elect my brother as the first Black justice of the peace in Smith County, Tyler, TX. She died the following year at 100 years of age.

Quincy Beavers (grandson), Joyce Dunlap ("Granny")
and, Election Judge Lowell Starling
(Photo courtesy of Beverly Beavers-Brooks)

My mother, Ophelia Jeffrey Beavers Daniels, was clearly, her mother's daughter. She was a strong, independent woman whose number one priority was caring for my brother and me. She got married at seventeen and moved to San Diego with my dad who had been drafted during World War II. When the war was over, they separated. My mother wanted to return to Texas and my dad wanted to live in California.

When Mother returned to Texas, she immediately enrolled in beauty school. After graduation, she opened her own business where she trained and mentored the stylists that she hired to work in the salon. She co-founded the Progressive Club of Cosmetology and served as its first president. As president, she brought the State Convention of the Texas Association of Beauty Culturists to Tyler. In 1982, she received an award from the Tyler chapter of the Negro Business and Professional Women's Clubs for outstanding contributions to women in business. In 1984, I received the Outstanding Entrepreneur Award from the Dallas Chapter of this organization.

Mother worked long hours so that my brother and I could have the best of what the world had to offer. Even with the long hours, however, she recognized the importance of having a balanced life. That balance included working in her church and serving the community in various ways through social and civic organizations.

From a very early age, I remember feeling the love my mother had for me and, as I grew up, I observed her love and compassion for others. I was a little girl of a darker hue and other kids would sometimes call me "black" in a derogatory manner. When I went to my mother crying, she would respond "The blacker the berry the sweeter juice. You are my sweet, beautiful little girl." She would dress me in bright colors to ensure that I always stood out in a crowd. She never stopped building up my self-esteem and confidence. Mother was my greatest promoter! She told me that I could be anything I chose to be and that she would always be there to support me. I never wanted to disappoint my mother. Whatever I have become in life is because of her. She was not only my mother, but she was also my best friend.

Beverly with her mother, Mrs. Ophelia Beavers Daniels
(Photo courtesy of Beverly Beavers-Brooks)

My mother and grandmother gave me the cornerstones of faith, service, and love of family, which are my most treasured legacies. These have become the reference points of my total existence. Whatever I have accomplished in life as an entrepreneur, public servant, social and political activist, and community volunteer, is a result of their example as well as the confidence they had in me, the resilience they instilled in me, and the independence they developed in me.

Beverly Beavers-Brooks
Tyler, TX

Beverly (Lyle) Brooks
(Photo courtesy of Beverly Brooks)

Beverly Beavers-Brooks (formerly Lyle) was born in Tyler, TX, and moved back after retirement in 2012. She has devoted her career and her retirement to being a community servant. Beverly's career spanned some forty-plus years. Many of the positions she held provided an opportunity for her to have a positive impact on the lives of others, especially women and minorities. The first such position was with the Minority Women's Employment Program (MWEP) which operated in ten cities nationwide. MWEP was a federally funded program that came under the auspices of R-T-P, Incorporated, a national non-profit organization. The mission of MWEP was to place college-degreed minority women into professional, managerial, and technical positions in the private sector. During her employment with MWEP, she served as a Project Director, National Field Coordinator, and National Deputy Director. It was this experience that prepared her for all career endeavors going forward.

The entrepreneurship bug that Beverly inherited from her mother and grandmother struck in the 1980s when she started and ran a telephone answering service business for seven years. After selling the business, she was hired by NCNB National Bank (which eventually became Bank of America) as the first Community Investment Officer in Dallas, TX, and was eventually promoted to Senior Vice President. She also served as the Community Investment Officer in Charlotte, NC at the Corporate Headquarters, and Regional Community Investment Officer in Atlanta, GA with responsibility for GA, FL, TN, and KY. While at Bank of America, she facilitated the development of products and services to meet the needs of low and moderate-income communities and small business customers.

Beverly's last positions before retirement were with the U.S. Department of Labor's Women's Bureau where she served as both the National Manager of

Field Operations and as Regional Administrator for Region VI with responsibility for TX, LA, AR, OK, and NM.

Other career and life experience highlights included participation as the youngest delegate in a study group to Israel led by civil rights activist Bayard Rustin in 1977; completed the Senior Executives in Government Fellows Program, Harvard University 2005; completed the Intensive Executive Spanish Program at Universidad Internacional-Center for Bilingual Multicultural Studies in Cuernavaca, Morelos, Mexico; and represented the United States at the International Labor conference in Geneva, Switzerland in 2009 as the lead delegate on Gender Equality.

In retirement, Beverly co-founded Friends Giving Back, Inc., a 501c3 nonprofit that raised and donated funds to organizations that served the needs of African Americans in her community. Beverly also manages several other nonprofits including the Emmett J. Scott Reunion Foundation and the Judge Quincy Beavers, Jr. Foundation to provide scholarships for deserving African American students. She has also remained very active in the political process with an emphasis on education and voter registration.

Beverly is a member of the National Council of Negro Women, Inc. and serves on its national board. Beverly is a 2000 graduate of Leadership Texas, a member of the Links, Inc., and Alpha Kappa Alpha Sorority, Inc. She has received numerous awards and recognition for her service to others.

Mrs. Richardine Barker

with daughters Dinetta Duncan, Jerralyn Winston, and Jeanine Oliga
(Photo courtesy of Dr. Jeanine Oliga)

"She had to walk down the street to get groceries, cook, feed the boys, wash dishes, do the laundry, and clean the house. Before going to school herself, she had to catch the bus and carry her youngest brother to daycare."

— Jeanine Barker Oliga, M.D., MPH

HONORING

Mrs. Richardine Barker

Written by Jeanine Barker Oliga, M.D., MPH / Daughter

I believe life can be sweet and that a lot goes into making it so. If it were not for my faith, I'm not sure how my life would have turned out. I credit my mom and dad for nurturing my gift of faith and I am forever grateful to them. They lovingly and carefully guided my siblings and me through this roller coaster called "life." For my three sisters and me, our mom, Mrs. Richardine Barker, has been a pillar of strength, in so many ways, and on many levels. She has been our inspiration, steadfast supporter, and constant encourager!

When my mom was fifteen, she already had a tremendous amount of responsibility. Her father started a newspaper business in Houston, TX, and her mother, also a strong woman of faith, worked tirelessly as a registered nurse. Given the nature of her parents' jobs, young Richardine was primarily responsible for her three younger brothers. She had to walk down the street to get groceries, cook, feed the boys, wash dishes, do the laundry, and clean the house. Before going to school herself, she had to catch the bus and carry her youngest brother to daycare. This meant that she had to be disciplined, selfless, tenacious, and strong. She did all this while also taking care of herself and doing her schoolwork. This history is important because this is what made Richardine the person that she is today.

So, just what kind of person is Mrs. Richardine Barker? First and foremost, she is "Mama" to me. Let me expound on what that means for my siblings and me. Our mom has remained faithful to God while joyfully raising five children. She has shown love to her husband and the entire family through her hard work and enduring commitment over the years. She has been a dedicated music teacher, a faithful member and diligent worker in the church, and a loyal member of her beloved Alpha Kappa Alpha Sorority, Inc. She has been the wind beneath the wings of five college graduates: three from Howard University, one from Morehouse College, and one from Florida A&M University. This was a major accomplishment but, because of the responsibility that she had and the strength she gained as a young girl, she was up to the task. Her children have gone on to have successful careers: an engineer, a corporate executive, a naval warfare officer and pilot, a banking and finance officer, a physical therapist, a medical doctor, and an educator and non-profit manager. They cover almost the entire spectrum of human services. It was her encouragement and support that made this possible.

Her influence on her children's lives has been evident in many ways. The following are a few of my sisters' favorite memories and examples of Mom's devotion, support, protection, and enduring love.

Jeanine Oliga and her mother, Mrs. Richardine Barker
(Photo courtesy of Dr. Jeanine Oliga)

Dinetta Duncan is my oldest sister. After her first year in college, Dinetta was blessed with a summer job at IBM in Boca Raton, FL. Mom used her sorority contacts to find a safe home for Dinetta to live in while she did her summer internship. At first, she took the bus to work but soon made friends with other interns, one of whom lived very close to where she was staying. Dinetta began to ride to work with this intern who did not hesitate to start sharing details about her wild life of drugs and sex. Dinetta was stunned but listened intently to these stories about things that she had only seen on TV. She told Mom about the conversation and the next day Mom arrived in Boca Raton with my dad's car in tow. Dinetta was to use this car to drive to work for the rest of that summer!

Jerralyn Winston is the middle child of the five. When she was in her last year of college, she became very sick with strep throat. Realizing how close she was to graduating, Mom was concerned that this illness might be a setback and could even affect her ability to graduate in good standing. So, Mom immediately arranged a flight to Washington, DC. She stayed at Jerri's bedside, waiting on her hand and foot, caring for her and, singing and listening with her to their favorite gospel songs until Jerri fully recovered. From this point on, Jerri never doubted that Mom always had her back.

I am the third daughter. From my perspective, Mom inspired in me a tremendous amount of self-confidence. When I was learning to drive, I remember that she was in the car but was reading the newspaper. I was shocked! She knew that I had never been behind the wheel of a car, yet she was cool, calm, and collected. I wondered, "Does she realize that I have never done this before?" I finally accepted that she was calm because she had the utmost confidence in me. She knew that I was observant and careful and that I would have studied the driver's booklet as well as her and my father's actions as they drove. Today, when I face challenges in life, I remember this experience and appreciate the faith in God and the confidence that my mother continues to inspire in me.

Mrs. Richardine Barker, Mom, is our inspiration, our steadfast supporter, our cheerleader, and our eternal love! My sisters and I aspire daily to be women cut from her mold. We are grateful and blessed to have her as our mother.

Jeanine Barker Oliga, M.D., MPH
Houston, TX

Dr. Jeanine Oliga
(Photo courtesy of Jeanine Oliga)

Jeanine Barker Oliga, M.D., MPH, a native of Houston, TX, received her medical degree from Morehouse School of Medicine and completed her residency at Morehouse Family Practice Residency. While at Morehouse, Dr. Oliga was the recipient of the Outstanding Academic Achievement in Maternal and Child Health Award. Oliga earned her Master of Public Health degree in

Health Administration from Emory University. She earned a Bachelor of Science degree in Physical Therapy from Howard University where she subsequently worked as an instructor in the Department of Physical Therapy.

Dr. Oliga was named to Who's Who in Black America, is a member of the National Alumni Association at Morehouse School of Medicine, and is a Life Member of Alpha Kappa Alpha Sorority, Inc. She and her husband, John, were 2011 Gloster Members at Morehouse School of Medicine. Dr. Oliga currently travels the country performing specialized health exams for targeted populations, including veterans.

Jeanine is happily married to Dr. John Oliga, a practicing internist. They have three adult children, Camille, Catherine, and John II, who are a true source of joy in her life.

Mrs. Alice Coats

(Photo courtesy of Jacqueline James)

"Many were afraid to participate in these sessions because of the possibility of losing their jobs or retaliation from the Knights of the Ku Klux Klan. My grandmother, on the other hand, was fearless!"

— Jacqueline "Jackie" James

HONORING

Mrs. Alice Coats and Mrs. Tesse Grimes Jackson

Written by Jacqueline "Jackie" James / Daughter and Granddaughter

As I reflect on my sixty-seven years of life, I sometimes wonder where I get my strength from: strength to sustain obstacles, stay grounded, and never allow myself to lose faith in God. Is it in my genes or could angels be surrounding me? After much deliberation, I now realize it's a little of both—heredity and angels.

My mother and grandmother were the most important people in my life. They guided and protected me when I knew nothing about life during adolescence or what life had to offer. Most importantly, they provided wise and compassionate guidance when I encountered difficult times as a young adult.

My mother, Alice Coats, was an educator and had a deep passion for helping students learn. She allowed no one to feel inferior even if their friends learned at a faster pace. She took her students' learning personally; staying after school to help them and taking extra measures to teach those children who needed additional help. I watched this and thought, "What a commitment to excellence." As a young child, I often asked myself, "Why is she doing this? She is not being paid to do this. Why do more than is required?" I later realized that it was not about the money, it was about care and commitment. She cared for the students and felt that if she did not give them a chance to succeed, they may never be given a chance. At some point, I realized that I wanted to imitate this type of excellence in my life.

As I watched my mother manage a career and raise me with little financial support after she divorced my dad, I became committed to the excellence that she modeled. During that time, the school system in Mississippi was the lowest-paying in the United States. Mother was determined that, during this time of racial division (1956-1974), I would not be denied a quality education. She sometimes borrowed books from others so that I could read more and experience different levels of learning. Her determination to take care of me inspired me at an early age to have the same determination to reach my goals and care for those that I love.

My mother believed in honest work, and she believed in me. Even as a full-time teacher, she found ways to generate more income for us. I learned from this as I observed her and when I entered college, I thought it was normal to have more than one job. Mother was a firm believer in financial stability and saving for a rainy day. I am the same. I have worked hard to achieve and maintain financial stability. She taught me how to do that. She lovingly ensured I had everything I needed and some of what I wanted. At sixty-seven, I have never had a toothache because dental care started for me at age five, eye care at age five also, and general health care from birth. Mother's priorities were in the right place. I also try to ensure that my priorities are in the right place. She taught me that.

Jackie James and her mom, Mrs. Alice Coats
(Photo courtesy of Jackie James)

Mother worked extremely hard in our small town of Philadelphia, MS to get African Americans registered to vote. She even picked many of our neighbors up and drove them to the courthouse to vote. She went to City Council meetings and fought for the hiring of African American policemen and policewomen. She also fought to get better roads in the African American community. She was recognized by the City of Philadelphia for her dedicated service and commitment to justice and the betterment of the community. This spirit of community and justice is in me also.

Mother's love for her mother forced her to retire so that she could take care of her. She also lovingly did what she could to help and support her sister when she needed it. She supported and encouraged me and was always there for me when I needed an extra dose of love or someone to listen to me. Mother has lovingly taken care of me through all my medical and health crises as I battle multiple sclerosis, and now, I take care of her.

Mother has made me the woman that I am today!

Mother I Love You!

Tesse Jackson and her granddaughter, Jackie James (left) Tesse Jackson and her daughter, Alice Coats, mother of Jackie James (right) (Photo courtesy of Jackie James)

My grandmother, Tessie Grimes Jackson, was born in 1913 and had very little education. As a teenager, she began working as a maid and babysitter for Caucasian families. She eventually became an entrepreneur because she knew that working for others was not something she wanted to do. She saved enough money to open and own a thriving grocery store where she sold a variety of commodities. She often allowed patrons to buy on credit so that they could feed their families until they received their next paycheck. Our community resembled a small Black Wall Street with rows of Black stores and even a very mini-hotel. I watched as she served and catered to the people of our little community. I saw her strength and admired her courage and leadership.

During the early '60s, Grandmother served civil rights workers who descended on Philadelphia to educate, register African Americans to vote, and help the community understand that their rights as citizens were the same as those of any U.S. citizen, regardless of race or creed. Many were afraid to participate in these sessions because of the possibility of losing their jobs or retaliation from the Knights of the Ku Klux Klan. My grandmother, on the other hand, was fearless!

Grandmother Tessie introduced me to Michael Schwerner, James Chaney, and Andrew Goodman, the three civil rights workers murdered in Philadelphia, MS in 1964. She was a woman of great faith. Her fearless attitude and faith had a tremendous impact on my life. I will never forget the Greyhound bus ride we took together in 1961 to Wilmington, NC. One of the stops that we made was in Birmingham, AL. Grandmother decided that we should go to the lunch counter to order a sandwich. When we got there, we were rudely asked "What do y'all want?" My grandmother boldly said, "My granddaughter and I would like a sandwich." The waitress responded: "We do not usually serve colored people in here." There were only white customers at the lunch counter. Showing no fear, my grandmother repeated, "We would like a sandwich." The waitress turned angrily and went to the grill to make the sandwiches which she, of course, threw our way when she was done. Grandmother paid, and we left.

As we walked away to eat the sandwiches, I asked Grandmother if she was afraid that we would be hurt. She replied with a smile, "No, God was with us, and He protects all who love him." I often think about the courage she had during a time when water fountains in the South were still labeled "Colored" and "White." To this day, that experience still encourages me to rely on God's love and protection in the face of challenges. I stand on Grandmother's shoulders, and I remember and try to channel her courage when I experience adversity.

Grandmother loved to cook, and I do too. Many of the dishes that I still prepare are her recipes. She was never a big talker and I'm not either. Our personalities were very similar. We often spent the whole day together saying very little. Both of us loved quiet time and just being together. One of the most important things that I learned from my grandmother was entrepreneurship. I owned a beauty salon for twenty years. And, like my mother, I did this while also holding a full-time job. I cherish these memories and the time we spent together. She taught me to be strong, believe in myself, help others, and put all my trust in God.

She always wore beautiful hats and sewed most of her clothes without using a pattern. I wish I had inherited that skill.

Grandmother was fearless, courageous, and faithful. I am as well!

I Love You, Grandmother!

Jacqueline "Jackie" James
Decatur, GA

Jacqueline "Jackie" James
(Photo courtesy of Jacqueline James)

Jacqueline "Jackie" James graduated from Morris Brown College in Atlanta with a bachelor's degree in Speech Communications. She has also earned a Sustainable Professional certificate from the Green Education Foundation Institute. Jackie is currently Director of Administrative Services at Spelman College with responsibility for managing the college's operational support functions including procurement, mail services, telecommunications, equipment leasing, and contract negotiations. She has served in that position for nearly twenty years and is a highly-respected and professional leader. Jackie served as Chair of Spelman's Leadership Council for seven years and chaired the development team for its first Process Mapping initiative.

While working at Spelman, Jackie also owned a beauty salon for twenty years. She has mentored many young women at Spelman and facilitated their access to financial aid.

Before her current position, Jackie was Director of Procurement Services for Blue Cross/Blue Shield, National Director of Purchasing and Distribution for Rollins Protective Services, and a procurement officer for Gourmet Services.

Jackie is a member of Alpha Kappa Alpha Sorority, Inc. She has been a Trustee at Mt. Patmos Baptist Church for fifteen years.

"Without faith, nothing is possible.
With it, nothing is impossible."

Dr. Mary McLeod Bethune

Mrs. Ruth Daniels

(Photo courtesy of Letetia Jackson)

"Mama got on her knees right there in the bank and prayed fervently to the Lord."

— Letetia Daniels Jackson

HONORING

Mrs. Ruth Daniels

Written by Letetia Daniels Jackson / Daughter

From the time I entered this world, my mom was special to me. I clung to her. My mom, Ruth Daniels, was a single mother who raised five kids. I am the youngest. She worked hard, but she made it look easy to this little girl who was always watching. Mama had a strong faith and that faith carried her, opened doors that seemed closed, healed my sister when the doctors had no hope, and sent my oldest brother to college without money. God always made a way for her.

When my brother said he wanted to go to college, Mom was determined to make a way. She went to a local bank for a loan to pay for his tuition and expenses. With five kids, no collateral, without owning a home or even a car, she went to the bank. She was told that without collateral, she could not get a loan. She responded, "My boy wants to go to college, and I want him to go and make something of himself." The bank officer listened and humored her, all the while knowing that he was not going to loan her money. In the middle of this discussion, he was called away and left her in his office. Mama got on her knees right there in the bank and prayed fervently to the Lord. When the banker returned, his whole demeanor had changed! My mom left that bank with more than she had asked for and my brother went to Stillman College in Tuscaloosa, AL, and graduated in 1970. I was at her side and witnessed the entire discussion and transaction. My mom taught me that *"Prayer changes things."* When you go with God, that's all you need. I never doubted that.

I was about six years old when my sister, Lenice, learned she had a tumor behind her right eye. It started to grow and began causing her eye to protrude. My mom was determined to get her the best medical help available. She heard about a good specialist in Mobile, AL so, she took Lenice there. The doctors attempted to reduce the tumor, but it was not effective. They told my mom to take my sister home and fatten her up because she had lost too much weight. They wanted her to be strong enough to endure the surgery. Mama was told that the surgery would be dangerous and could render my sister blind. My mom came home with my sister and asked everyone she knew to pray for Lenice.

I witnessed Mama on her knees many nights praying fervently to the Lord to heal my sister. She believed the Lord would answer her prayer. She never doubted and she never gave up hope. When Mama took Lenice back to Mobile, the doctors ran tests and took

X-rays to prepare for surgery. And you know what? They could not find the tumor! The tumor that had been causing my sister's eye to protrude; the tumor that was wrapped around her optic nerve and could have been damaged during surgery leaving her blind, could not be found on any X-ray. The doctors were astonished. My mom wasn't. She had prayed for my sister's total and complete healing, and she believed that God would hear her prayer. The tumor had miraculously disappeared. It was gone. There was no trace of it! Anywhere!

This experience sealed my faith in the Lord and from that day forward, I have never doubted the power of the Lord. And my mom? Well, I put her in the category of my living saint. Throughout my life, whenever I needed a prayer answered, I called my mom. Her prayer was always answered. I would call Mama before an important speech, a presentation at work, a job interview, when facing medical concerns, and for various other trials and tribulations, and her prayers always got through. Always! The greatest gift that my mom gave to me was the gift of faith. The gift of having a personal relationship with the Lord. It carries me through any situation.

Mama also gave me the gift of resiliency. Whenever I am faced with a challenge or trial that seems too difficult to bear, I think about her and I tell myself: "If Mama could raise five kids alone, send to college all who wanted to go, feed us, keep a roof over our heads, and clothes on our backs with little help from anyone, then I can get through this." I then laugh at my challenge. It was always small in comparison. Because of my mom and the life lessons I learned watching her, I believe I can do anything and can overcome anything. And guess what? I have. I have accomplished remarkable goals and overcome every obstacle. I have seen and experienced things that this little girl from McRae Homes in Dothan, AL never even knew was imaginable!

Mama worked a job, sold Avon, and sewed, making most of our clothing growing up. I learned to sew sitting at her side (which is where I always was), watching everything she did. I was such a good student that, one year later, I made an entire suit, complete with a matching tie. It was my brother's Easter suit. When we needed extra money, Mama baked sweet potato pies and sold them. They always sold out quickly. In her final years, she told me that my sweet potato pie was "almost as good as hers." She would say to me: "You almost got me, girl!" That was the highest honor she could have given me. What's funny though, is that every year at Thanksgiving when I called her for the recipe, she always added one new ingredient. When I called her out, she would say "Well, I can't give you all my secrets at once!" I don't think I ever got the full recipe!

I am the woman I am today because of my mom. I have a strong personal relationship with the Lord and a strong, impenetrable faith because of her. Because of her, I believe that I can do anything I put my mind to.

Once I became a teenager, I changed, as teenagers do. I wanted to be with my friends more than with my mom. That broke her heart. She never wanted me to grow up. Even after I went off to college, graduated, started to work, and traveled the world, I remained her baby girl. In her eyes, I never grew up. She is no longer with me on earth, but I still cherish the thought of being her baby girl.

Letetia Jackson and her mother, Mrs. Ruth Daniels
(Photo courtesy of Letetia Jackson)

I left Dothan for college at seventeen, two months after graduating from high school. But as my mom aged, I moved back home to be closer to her. That was the greatest gift I could have given her. We shared eighteen of my adult years and I did my best to spoil her as much as she spoiled me.

When I decided to become a plaintiff in the 2022 successful Supreme Court Case, Allen v. Milligan, the lawsuit against the State of Alabama's discriminatory redistricting congressional map, I did so with her in mind. I was the only one on our team who believed that we were going to win the case. I never wavered in that belief, not once. When I listened to Justice Ketanji Brown Jackson question the Alabama solicitor and watched her take her colleagues to school regarding the Founders' original intent for the 14th and 15th Amendments, my belief that we would succeed was solidified! It matters to have a seat at the table. I know Mama was smiling down from heaven as she watched me sitting in the Supreme Court with a Black female Justice of the Court.

Letetia Jackson and her mother, Mrs. Ruth Daniels
(Photo courtesy of Letetia Jackson)

I still remember when my mom was able to register and vote for the first time. She took voting seriously and always took me with her. She only missed voting once in her later years because she was not able to go. She was very proud to be able to vote twice for President Barack Obama. Her last vote was for President Joe Biden in the primary. She was in heaven for the general election. She instilled that same level of serious responsibility for voting in my siblings and me. So, to become a part of a case that was about making sure our vote and our voice counted was a natural progression for me. I became involved in honor of her.

Even though she's gone to heaven, she lives on through me. I am her. I am my mother's daughter. I am my mother. Nothing can top that!

Letetia "Tish" Daniels Jackson
   Dothan, AL

Letetia "Tish" Jackson
(Photo courtesy of Letetia Jackson)

Letetia Daniels Jackson is President/CEO of Tandeka LLC, a strategic consulting firm specializing in authentic community and civic engagement, public policy advocacy, government relations, strategic planning, and capacity building for non-governmental organizations. She is recognized nationally for successful policy advocacy campaigns in the Southern Region that resulted in significant policy and systems changes. She is the convener of the South Alabama Black Women's Roundtable, an affiliate of the National Coalition on Black Civic Participation (NCBCP) Black Women's Roundtable that serves as the intergenerational leadership development, mentoring, empowerment, and power-building arm for Black women and girls.

Letetia is one of the plaintiffs in Allen v. Milligan, where on June 8, 2023, the Supreme Court of the United States ruled in favor of the Milligan Plaintiffs in holding that Alabama's 2021 congressional redistricting plan violated Section 2 of the Voting Rights Act. As a result, a special master appointed by the District Court drew the map that created the new 2nd Congressional District giving Black voters a plurality and an opportunity to elect a representative of their choice to represent them in Congress in 2025.

Currently, Letetia serves as Tandeka's Project Director for the Robert Wood Johnson Foundation's (RWJF) $6.5 million program initiative, Building Capacity to Reduce Tobacco Inequities in the South and Midwest, a program designed to increase the ability of African Americans, persons of lower socio-economic status, and rural residents to advocate for stronger, local, or regional tobacco control and reduced usage. Tandeka has also worked with Campaign for Tobacco-Free Kids in Mississippi and Louisiana.

Letetia served as program director for Groundswell Fund to implement their Integrated Voter Engagement Program and has served as Director for the

Campaign for Tobacco-Free Kids in the southern region, National Campaign Manager for NCBCP's Unity 2012 Campaign, National Field Director for the Unity 2010 Campaign, consultant to NCBCP's 2010 Decennial Census Unity Diaspora Coalition, and served on the Advisory Board for Ford Foundation-funded Praxis Project's Building Capacity Building Power Initiative.

Ms. Jackson is Chair of the Board of Directors for Women Engaged, serves on the boards of Alabama Forward, the HBCU Green Fund, and is a board member and treasurer of Dothan Downtown Redevelopment Authority. Letetia serves on RWJF's Culture of Health Prize National Advisory Committee, the RWJF Policy Advocacy Evaluation Advisory Committee, and the RWJF/American Heart Association Voices for Healthy Kids Evaluation Advisory Committee.

Letetia holds a B.A. in Finance from Georgia State University and is currently a Juris Doctor student at the American Institute of Law. She is married to Michael B. Jackson and is an active member of Dothan Community Church.

Mrs. Velma Hadessa Wilson Norvel

(Photo courtesy of Paulette Lewis)

*"God ordered my steps in answer
to my mother's prayers."*

— Paulette Norvel Lewis

HONORING

Mrs. Velma Hadessa Wilson Norvel

Written by Paulette Norvel Lewis / Daughter

My mother was a wise and beautiful woman of faith. Faith was her first and most precious legacy to my siblings and me. Mama was the only child of a single mother. She grew up in Chicago, but her mother sent her to Pascagoula, MS to spend summers with her Godmother so that young Velma would not be home alone while she worked. When she became a teenager, Velma made a pact with God to give Him her firstborn if He would allow her to live in Pascagoula where she had developed friends her age and would not be confined at an apartment all day. God took her up on that promise. On the day that her firstborn and only son was ordained a priest, she casually shared this promise with our family. It is a powerful testimony of Mama's faith and prayers.

Being a wife, and mother, and having a family of her own was the fulfillment of Mama's dreams. My father, one of thirteen children, was also a man of faith. Marrying into his large, close, faith-filled, and loving family gave Mama a sense of belonging and filled her heart with joy. Even though my parents were originally of different religious denominations, there was no difference in their faith in God's mercy, forgiveness, love, and care in every circumstance of their lives. They were not "in your face" with their faith however, it was evident in their behavior and how they treated others. They were a joyful and generous couple, and my friends and our extended family often visited just to be around them. Even though we had very little, they did not hesitate to share the little we had with others who were in need. One of my cousins once commented to me: "I never worry about Aunt Velma and Uncle Willie. It seems that the Lord always takes care of them."

My mother had a ninth-grade education, and my father had a sixth-grade education. So, in addition to having a family, making sure that we had a good education, was the primary motivation of Mama's work life. She worked very hard doing domestic work, and eventually as a public school cafeteria manager to earn enough money to pay Catholic school tuition. When the school that my siblings attended closed, she searched fervently to find a "Black" Catholic school that I could attend. The Catholic school less than a mile from our home was not integrated.

My brother shared my mother's concern with his seminary classmate from Mobile, AL who recommended that she contact Mrs. Gloria Caponis. Ms. Caponis was a single mother and educator with a daughter my age who would be attending Most Pure Heart of Mary High School in Mobile. My mother did not know her however, she reached out in faith to contact her. Mrs. Caponis generously agreed to allow me to stay with her in Mobile (nearly fifty miles away from my home) during the week and return home on weekends. Although it was difficult to let her youngest child leave home at such a young age, Mama knew that in the long run, it would be best for me. We did not always have a reliable car so, if my parents could not pick me up, I had to take the Greyhound bus home.

Paulette's classmates at Heart of Mary High School

This arrangement changed the entire trajectory of my life! Not only was I able to go to Heart of Mary High School, but I received a full college scholarship to Edgewood College in Madison, WI, which is owned and operated by the Catholic Sisters who taught at HOM. Heart of Mary was a wonderful community of smart, talented, motivated African American youth and their committed, progressive, and loving teacher-mentors. It gave me a sense of belonging, was emotionally and socially supportive, and ignited my interest in, and advocacy for civil rights as a Christian responsibility to "love my neighbor as myself." At Heart of Mary, I gained lifelong friends and, more importantly, a sister. The teenage daughter of Mrs. Caponis with whom I lived and went to school was Alexis Herman, the 23rd U. S. Secretary of Labor. We have worked together, played, supported, and loved one another as sisters for over sixty years.

Mrs. Velma Norvel (left) and daughter, Paulette Lewis
(Photo courtesy of Paulette Lewis)

More importantly, Heart of Mary didn't just give me lifelong friends, it gave me my husband of thirty-four years, Marion Lewis. Although we didn't really know one another as classmates, through our connections with Alexis, we met again years later. Our shared values, faith, friends, high school experience, willingness to serve, and love of family, created an enduring bond of love and devotion. God ordered my steps on many levels because of my mother's persistence and prayers. Prayer was her superpower.

Marion and Paulette Lewis

Mama also wanted us to know that there were opportunities and life outside of small-town Pascagoula so, she allowed us to travel and encouraged us to embrace new experiences whenever possible. My sisters went by train to Chicago to visit our grandmother. Because I was much younger than my sisters, I only traveled with my mother. We went to a Ladies Auxiliary of Saint Peter Claver convention in Washington, D.C. where she served as a delegate, and to Reno, Nevada to visit her best friend who had recently given birth to twins that she named after my parents, William, and Velma. These experiences were empowering, and, as a result, my siblings and I all developed a love of travel.

Mama worked and served in the church as a member of the Ladies Auxiliary of the Knights of St. Peter Claver (KPC), cleaned the church, ironed church linens, and made her delicious gumbo for the church bazaar. For many years, she was the Counselor for the Junior Daughters of KPC, providing guidance for young girls and directing their community service projects. She served as a poll worker, worked for voter registration, and voted regularly in local and national elections. Like her, I have spent most of my career working to empower women and girls with jobs and educational opportunities, advocating for civil rights, and working in the church.

Whatever my mother did, she did wholeheartedly, well, and without fanfare. Whether she was cleaning the local White women's social club, sewing, cooking for her family, cleaning houses, or managing the public school cafeteria, everyone knew that if Velma did it, it would be done well and on time. Her word was her bond. Mama taught us that if something is worth doing, it's worth doing well. If we did something sloppily, we were reminded that: "Haste makes waste." We learned from her example that doing work well not only saved time (because it did not have to be "cleaned up" later) but it reflected our self-respect and the regard we have for those we serve. It is also a way of honoring our God-given talents and skills. I also aspire to be a person of my word and to do my work with excellence.

In his book, *The Prophet*, Khalil Gibran expressed it very simply: "Work is love made visible." Doing her work with excellence was one of my mother's "love languages." It became one of mine as well.

My sisters and I learned many other beautiful lessons from my mother. We learned to laugh freely and often, to love and trust God, to appreciate and acknowledge the accomplishments of others, to have a heart full of gratitude, and to value family.

Mrs. Velma Norvel (left) and daughter, Paulette Lewis
(Photo courtesy of Paulette Lewis)

I miss laughing together as we shopped for greeting cards, holding hands as we walked through the mall (even as adults), her melodious laugh, her warm hazel eyes, and her cooking, especially the gumbo! I miss HER and I love her.

Paulette Norvel Lewis
Atlanta, GA

Paulette Norvel Lewis
(photo by Jacqueline James, courtesy of Paulette Lewis)

Paulette Norvel Lewis has had a forty-year career working in private industry and non-profit organizations as a career development professional providing employment assistance, career counseling, and coaching for women and girls. In the 1970s, she and The Honorable Alexis Herman co-founded the Minority Women Employment Program in Atlanta, GA. The organization expanded to ten major U.S. cities and successfully placed over 2,500 women of color in management, technical, and professional jobs in private industry.

Ms. Lewis established the first Training and Safety Program for the City of Atlanta in the 1980s, she served as Chief of Staff for Mrs. Coretta Scott King and worked directly with Dr. Dorothy Height as Interim Executive Vice President of the National Council of Negro Women (NCNW). She served twenty-one years in the federal government including six years as Regional Advocate of the Small Business Administration, a presidential appointment of President Clinton. From there, she went to the U.S. Department of Labor as Chief of Discretionary Programs where she managed 400 million dollars of federal grants around the southeast. She retired in 2014 after serving eight years as Regional Administrator of the Women's Bureau, U, S, Department of Labor, Region IV.

Ms. Lewis has been recognized locally and nationally for her advocacy for pay equity and equal employment opportunities for women and STEAM educational opportunities for girls. She is a member of Leadership Atlanta, the YWCA Academy of Women Achievers, and Alpha Kappa Alpha Sorority, Inc. She received the POW! Award from Womentics, a "Trailblazer" Award from Congressman Hank Johnson, an Outstanding Achievement Award from President William Jefferson Clinton for her work on the White House Conference on Small Business, a Lifetime Achievement award from the U.S. Department of Labor and was named one of Atlanta's 100 Black Women of Influence. She has served as Chair of the Lyke House Catholic Student Center Advisory Board at Atlanta University Center and was on the founding board of the award-winning International Community School in Avondale, GA, a baccalaureate school founded for refugee and local children to foster the Beloved Community."

Ms. Lewis has a B.A. Degree in Education from Edgewood College in Madison, WI. She has always been inspired by the strength, resilience, creativity, and brilliance of "Black Girl Magic" which led her to compile this anthology, *My Mother's Daughter: A Heritage of Faith, Service, Wisdom, and Love.*

Paulette is currently a freelance writing consultant and career coach and serves on the National Council of Negro Women's Executive Board as Chair of the National Program Committee. She has co-authored two books, *Moving Up: Placing Minority Women in Private Industry* and *A Halleluia Song: Memoir of a Black Priest from the Jim Crow South.*

Mrs. Isabelle Juanita Smith Norvell

(Photo courtesy of Eleanor Tait)

"She gave the gift of music to our family, and it has continued through five generations."

— Eleanor Norvell Tait

HONORING

Mrs. Isabelle Juanita Smith Norvell ("Miz Belle")

Written by Eleanor Norvell Tait / Daughter

Isabelle Juanita Smith Norvell was born in 1922 to Walter and Ella Smith in Moss Point, MS. She united in holy matrimony to Harding Norvell of Pascagoula, MS. To this union four daughters were born: Ramona, Gertrude, Eleanor (me), and Walterine. I am my mother's daughter. Every time I walk past a mirror, I see her face. When combing my gray hair, I am immediately reminded that we nicknamed her the "Silver Fox" because of her beautiful silver-gray hair. And I cannot forget that I inherited that dreaded disease, arthritis, from which she also suffered.

As I observe the children or grandchildren of "Miz Belle" or "Granny" or "Granny Chick" (as her children and fourteen grandchildren referred to her), I see something of her in each of them. Miz Belle led not by the "example of her power but by the power of her example." It is hard to determine exactly where her descendants would be today if it were not for her deep love for God which emboldened her to be the strong and resilient woman, mother, grandmother, and friend she was throughout her eighty-one years of life. Her opinion, point of view, words, and nuggets of wisdom were not always adhered to when imparted but they landed on good soil because eventually, they yielded results. Her legacy includes fifteen preachers, ten musicians, teachers, bishops, CPAs, artists, nurses, engineers, and others with a plethora of gifts and talents.

We were never told what we could not do, and this empowerment continues to be passed on to each generation. The wisdom imparted from our mother included that we are here on purpose with God-given assignments: lessons to learn, work to do, and gifts to give which cannot be fulfilled if handicapped by attitudes and behaviors not in accord with the good that God intended. She instilled in us that we must use our innate gifts and talents, live on purpose, and most importantly, "carry our own heads" by not allowing others to impose their values on our lives. If there was a lesson she was trying to teach or a point she was making, you would have already seen it exemplified in her life. She didn't just talk. Though it has been twenty years since her transition, memories are immediately stirred when one of her grandchildren imparts a bit of her wisdom or humor to a great-grandchild who, unfortunately, did not experience her greatness firsthand.

In 1960, my mother changed her religious affiliation from the Methodist faith to a little holiness church, creating much dissension within her immediate family. The Church of the Living God consisted of a body of believers whose tenets and beliefs were vastly different from those of the Methodist tradition in which she was raised. However, this move opened a floodgate to God's overall gift and purpose for her life, the gift of music. She gave the gift of music to our family, and it has continued through five generations. One of her proudest moments was the creation of a singing group of her grandchildren, "The Norvellaires," a gift that, even today, keeps on giving. My mother not only shared the gift of music with her children, but she was also the youth advisor and musician at her new church and, was therefore able to share it with many other young people. It became abundantly clear to us that to sing or play sacred music was to "pray twice."

Mother served in many roles at her new church. She was a devoted member of the Women's Ministry, church secretary, and in any capacity where her gifts were needed. As her children, we were expected to do the same and participate in everything at church. A section of the Women's Ministry's pledge was to make "your home a center of love and light for Christ." Miz Belle did just that. This is something I have tried to emulate. Everyone was made to feel comfortable and treated with the utmost respect.

Family gatherings were the best of times. Sometimes it was just an impromptu Friday night fish fry that became a fun-filled party. Mother welcomed everyone into our home. I don't know of anyone else who invited a UPS driver in for a plate of food! Holidays were full of love, laughter, and food. Every one of her children and grandchildren and, of course, her best friends, received a Christmas gift from Granny. It did not matter what it was or that money was tight, it was a gift from Granny and an expression of her love! She was always giving of her time, talent, and treasure.

Miz Belle's work ethic at home and church was impeccable. Her desire to improve her economic situation led her in later years to enroll in a typing class. Completing this milestone allowed her to become more stable economically because it facilitated her being hired for a clerical position at Ingalls Shipbuilding. Acquiring clerical skills was the pathway from cleaning private homes to an office job with benefits and opportunities for upward mobility.

My mother did not flinch throughout the many adversities of her life. Her faith was her armor and it strengthened her to persevere. Whether standing, sitting, or walking, she was regal and stately. She was our matriarch. I recall a quote that described a strong woman as "both soft and powerful, practical and spiritual." That was my mother, my role model, and the woman that I aspire to emulate daily.

Some of my mother's grandchildren still reflect on their relationships with her. Randi recalls that Mom admonished her to stop using the words "I can't." Michelle believed that Miz Belle was the epitome of a person with grit. Sharron won't forget talking to Granny during their daily one-hour commute from work. Joseph said that he always enjoyed her company. Cedric won't forget that she took a group of her grandchildren and great-grandchildren, The Norvelliars, to WOSM, a predominantly White radio station, to sing. She was very proud of them and not at all apprehensive or intimidated by the experience.

Mother played and sang her favorite song every day: "When He calls me, I will answer. I'll be somewhere listening for my name." On April 15, 2004, at 6:30 a.m., the Lord called, and she answered. She has left wonderful memories and a living legacy of faith, service, love, and family.

Eleanor Norvell Tait
Moss Point, MS

The Norvell Clan, descendants of Mrs. Isabelle Norvell
Matriarchs, Gertrude Williams and Eleanor Tait, first row, center (Photo
courtesy of Eleanor Tait)

Mrs. Eleanor Tait
(Photo courtesy of Eleanor Tait)

Evangelist Eleanor Norvell Tait is the third daughter of Isabelle Norvell. She was recently widowed after fifty-five years of marriage to her wonderful husband, Alfred Louis Tait, Sr. Currently, the sparkle in her eye is for her three "perfect" children, Alfred, Jr., Ennis, and Michelle. Serving others and teaching the life-giving Word of God for over forty years is her greatest passion.

Eleanor worked as a personnel specialist at Ingalls Shipbuilding Corporation in Pascagoula, MS for thirty-nine years where she serviced the company's craftsmen. Twelve years into her retirement from Ingalls, Eleanor still happily encounters her many shipyard "children" as well as many of her church "children." Her own children describe Eleanor as a woman of integrity and tenacity. In their words: "I hit the parent lottery when Eleanor Norvell Tait gave birth to me."

Mrs. Thelma Triplett

and daughter, Danita Knight
(Photo courtesy of Danita Knight)

"Family, continue to be kind and thoughtful
to each other and all people. Continue to
put the Lord first in your lives."

— Danita Knight

Mrs. Thelma Gertrude Reeves Triplett

Written by Danita Knight / Daughter

I am pleased to introduce you to my amazing mother: Mrs. Thelma Gertrude Reeves Triplett. Mom lived to the "beyond blessed" age of ninety-two and spent her life living as a Proverbs thirty-one woman. I have chosen to introduce her to you based on excerpts from that scripture.

"Her price is far above rubies."
Everyone treasured Mom, those who knew her well, and strangers alike. She and my father fed people, allowed relatives in need to live with us, and practiced Christian hospitality daily. Several of my cousins received advanced degrees because Mom nurtured and supported them.

"The heart of her husband doth safely trust in her . . . she will do him good and not evil all the days of her life."
Mom was a minister's wife and a "first lady." The word "lady" was exactly what she exemplified. From wearing hats and gloves to her kind demeanor, Mom made my father and our family proud. We often had matching outfits that she made from scratch. We understood the value of having pride in our appearances and were always reminded to represent our family appropriately. And no one was prouder of Mom than our father!

"She seeks wool and flax and works willingly with her hands."
Mom worked full-time but managed to routinely sew clothes for me, my sister, and herself. She would often stay up late at night or rise early in the morning to make our clothes for trips, proms, Easter, and other special events. She also ensured that my sister and I had fresh "press and curls" for Sunday and other special events, and never got angry when we "sweated out our hair" from playing outside.

"She considers a field and buys it; with the fruit of her hands, she plants a vineyard . . . "
My parents moved us from the city of St. Louis to a nearby suburb when I was eleven years old. We were the first Black family in our neighborhood but were embraced by our neighbors when they got to know our parents. My sister, Sheila, now lives in our childhood home. Mom also routinely had a garden, with vegetables that we and neighbors enjoyed.

"She looks well to the ways of her household and eats not the bread of idleness."

Mom was always on time, immaculately dressed, and ensured that our family's needs were met. She was a planner and even designed her funeral program. Her last words were documented on the back of that program, where she shared, "I thank the Lord for a happy, long life with each of you, where I hope I left some meaningful memories that will be useful to each of you daily. If it is the Lord's will, I will always be with you in spirit. Family, continue to be kind and thoughtful to each other and all people. Continue to put the Lord first in your lives."

Danita Knight
Atlanta, GA

Danita Knight
(Photo courtesy of Danita Knight)

Danita V. Knight assumed the position of President and Chief Executive Officer for the YWCA of Greater Atlanta on January 3, 2023. She previously served as Vice President for Communications and Marketing at Agnes Scott College. Before joining Agnes Scott, Knight was a marketing, communications, public relations, and fundraising consultant for various non-profits, colleges, and political campaigns in Atlanta.

Ms. Knight is a past board chairperson of the Atlanta Women's Foundation (and the first Black board chair of that foundation). She was also chairperson of the 2007, 2009, 2010, and 2011 Atlanta Women's Foundation's "Numbers Too Big to Ignore" fundraising luncheons. The 2011 luncheon raised $1 million, at that time, the largest amount raised for a luncheon in the organization's history.

Other activities include Alpha Kappa Alpha Sorority, Inc., Vice-Chairperson of The Brookhaven Social Justice Race and Equity Commission, International Women's Forum-Georgia, the National Center for Civil and Human Rights Women's Solidarity Society, Advisory Board Member for Lending Hearts, a non-profit in Pittsburgh focused on recreational activities for adolescents with cancer, and various political campaigns and committees. Danita was part of the original group of "seed funders" responsible for bringing the women's professional basketball team, the WNBA Dream, to Atlanta.

Ms. Knight has also served as Vice President for Public Affairs and Community Relations at the National Collegiate Athletic Association (NCAA), Indianapolis, Indiana; Director of Public Relations at Anthem, Inc., Indianapolis, IN; Director of Communications for the Indianapolis Chamber of Commerce; Deputy Director for Communications and Public Affairs for the Council of State Governments, Lexington, KY; Director of Media and Public Relations for the United Way of Central Iowa, Des Moines, IA; assistant, speechwriter, scheduler, and public relations director to Iowa's first female Lieutenant Governor, Jo Ann Zimmerman; information specialist for the Iowa Commission on the Status of Women; and Public Relations Manager for the Iowa Department of Elder Affairs. She started her career as a student morning news anchor and reporter at KOMU-TV in Columbia, MO.

Knight is a graduate of the University of Missouri-Columbia, where she majored in broadcast (television) journalism. She lives in Atlanta with her husband, former Atlanta Hawks General Manager, Billy Knight. The Knights have two adult daughters, Erika and Olivia, and "wonderful grandchildren."

"My mother believed in education
like the devil believes in sin!"

Dr. Johnnetta Betsch Cole

Mrs. Mary Frances Betsch

(Photograph courtesy of Dr. Johnnetta Cole)

"However, my daughter, if anthropology is your passion, then you must pursue it!"

— Dr. Johnnetta Betsch Cole

HONORING

Mrs. Mary Frances Lewis Betsch

Written by Dr. Johnnetta Betsch Cole / Daughter

In the time-honored and powerful tradition of Black women's storytelling, here are stories about my mother, Mary Frances Lewis Betsch. These stories will not only capture who my mother was. They will clearly express how profoundly my mother shaped, influenced, and molded who I have become.

My mother supported my earliest commitment to social justice activism.
My mother was the granddaughter of Abraham Lincoln Lewis who was born in Madison County, FL to Judy and Robert Lewis, soon after they had been freed from enslavement. They named their child Abraham Lincoln Lewis to honor the fact that he was born in 1865, the year that President Abraham Lincoln declared an end to enslavement.

Abraham Lincoln Lewis (who preferred to be called A. L. Lewis) only had an elementary school education, but he became Florida's first Black millionaire. In 1901, he and six other prominent Black men in Jacksonville, FL founded the Afro-American Industrial and Benefit Association which later became the Afro-American Life Insurance Company. A.L. Lewis was the lead officer of "The Afro" when the company purchased over 250 acres on Amelia Island along the shore of the Atlantic Ocean in Florida to establish the historic American Beach Community. At that time, A. L. Lewis said that American Beach should be a place where his people could have recreation and relaxation without humiliation.

A. L. Lewis married Mary Frances Sammis, the great-granddaughter of Zephaniah Kingsley, a British enslaver, and Anta Madjiguene Ndiaye. When she was thirteen years old, Anta, who was of a royal Wolof family in Senegal, West Africa was captured. She was sent through the "Door of No Return" on Goree Island, and subjected to the brutalities of the Middle Passage. She was off-boarded in Havana Cuba, where she was bought by Zephaniah Kingsley, a British enslaver. He impregnated her before they reached his plantation in Florida.

Because of my mother's economic status in Jacksonville, FL she had privileges that countless Black people in her hometown did not have. One of those privileges was that periodically, a salesperson from the main department store in Jacksonville would call my mother and say: "Mrs. Betsch, we have just received some lovely new dresses. (Again, because of her economic status, she was not addressed as "Auntie" as so many Black women in that era were disrespectfully addressed.) "Please bring the girls to the store this evening after we are closed so that they can try them on." Why was there such a call to my mother? Because, during those despicable days of racial segregation, Black people could not try on clothes in department stores.

Abraham Lincoln ("A.L".) Lewis
(Photo of Dr. Johnnetta Cole)

Malvyne and Johnnetta Betsch (L)
The Residence of Mr. & Mrs. A.L. Lewis (R)
(Photographs courtesy of Dr. Johnnetta Cole)

One evening, when I was ten years old, and we were driving home from shopping in the department store after it had closed, I said to my mother: "Mama, if I cannot try on clothes in that store in the light of day, please I don't ever again want to try on clothes in the darkness of night."

My mother promised me that we would cease to be participants in that form of racial discrimination. She told us that she would either buy our clothes without our trying them on, even if they had to be exchanged, or we would be treated to clothes that we could try on when we traveled up north. My mother's defense of my stance against racism set me on my journey of becoming a social justice activist.

My mother believed in education like the devil believes in sin!

Unlike many African Americans in their generation, both of my parents were college graduates. And from the time that I was "knee-high to a duck," as the old folks in Jacksonville would say, my mother made sure that I obtained as much education as I possibly could. The reason this was necessary, she explained, (as so many Black mothers explained to their children) was that Black children had to be twice as good to get half as far as White children.

That is why I was sent to the first grade when I was five years old. Of course, in those days it was a "Colored Elementary School." When I was fifteen years old and had completed the 11th grade, my parents told me that I must go downtown in Jacksonville and take a test, and if I passed it, I would attend Fisk University in an early entrance program. I did not want to leave my family and my high school, but I knew I had to obey my parents. So, I took the test, and rather than just checking the wrong answers, like the "A" type that I was, I checked the right answers, and thus off I went to Fisk University at age fifteen. From Fisk, I went to Oberlin College where I received a bachelor's degree in sociology, and then on to graduate school at Northwestern to receive a master's and doctorate in anthropology.

Johnnetta Betsch at Fisk University (age 15)
(Photograph courtesy of Dr. Johnnetta Cole)

Years before I ever set foot in a school room, my mother told me that learning to read books and loving reading books was one of the most important things I must do. My mother and my teachers in the segregated schools that I attended helped me to develop a deep interest in what I was learning and how I was learning in school as well as in my everyday activities.

I also witnessed the joy my mother received from being a professor of English at Edward Waters College, an HBCU in our hometown, where she also served as the registrar. After my mother left Edward Waters College to work in our family's insurance business, I witnessed her commitment to lifelong learning. Among my most prized material possessions is a shelf of books in my library that were my mother's—sixty-two hard-covered books of classic works of literature.

My mother was clearly very influential in how I, at a very early age, acquired very positive ideas about scholarship and academia. Indeed, Mary Frances Lewis Betsch was a wonderful role model of how I could become a scholar, a professor, and a college administrator.

My mother believed, and she taught me to believe that "being of service to others is just the rent you have to pay for your room on earth."
Like all the members of my family, my mother believed in and put into practice a commitment to being of service to others. Thus, it was not surprising to me and my sister, and later it would not be surprising to our brother who was born nine years after I was born, that Mildred Olivia Tucker came to be our "adopted" big sister.

Melvyne, John Thomas, and Johnnetta Betsch
With Mildred Tucker (adult), their new "sister"
(Photo courtesy of Dr. Johnnetta Cole)

This is how that happened. One day, after my mother finished teaching her classes at Edward Waters College, she brought Mildred Tucker home with her. And, in a matter-of-fact voice, Mama said: "This is Milly Tucker, she is a student at Edward Waters. She is your new big sister who will live with us and help take care of you." And indeed, Milly did. Once she graduated from Edward Waters College, our parents sent Milly to Stanford University where she earned a master's degree and went on to work in administration at Bennett College.

My mother continuously brought into my life amazing Black women who she said I would do well to learn from her and should do my best to model my life after her. The most important of those sheroes in my life was Dr. Mary McLeod Bethune, who was introduced to me by my great-grandfather, A. L. Lewis. Indeed, A. L. Lewis and Dr. Bethune were colleagues and close friends who came to know each other well when she served on the board of Edward Waters College where A.L. Lewis was a trustee, and he served on the board of Bethune Cookman College where Dr. Bethune was the president.

As my mother drove my sister and me to Daytona Beach, FL where we would have the privilege of spending a little time with Dr. Bethune in her office, I remember asking her what she wanted me to learn from Dr. Bethune. She replied that I should learn about Dr. Bethune's humble beginnings, and I should appreciate the significance of what Dr. Bethune meant when said that the whole world opened up to her once she learned to read. My mother said I should listen to Dr. Bethune's story of how she not only founded a college, but also became a trusted advisor to American presidents, and founded the National Council of Negro Women. She told me that I was blessed to know and spend even a little time with Dr. Bethune. She assured me that one day I would fully appreciate that I had the privilege of knowing one of the greatest women in our country and the world, an amazing and grace-filled woman of faith who truly put into practice the saying that "Doing for others is just the rent you must pay for your room on earth."

My mother passed many years before I had the profound honor of serving as the 7th president and chair of the board of the National Council of Negro Women, an organization that was founded by Dr. Bethune eighty-nine years ago. But I believe that from her place in Glory, my mother knew that she <u>and</u> Dr. Bethune had prepared me to do that work.

My mother was a Black feminist in the sense that she taught me to follow my passion, and not to be dependent on a man for my livelihood.

I went off to Oberlin College with every intention of becoming a pediatrician—something I had said I wanted to be from an early age. But one day in an introduction to cultural anthropology class, I was so taken by what my professor described as the work of anthropologists that by the end of the class I was saying: "Goodbye pediatrics and hello anthropology!"

When I came home from school to Jacksonville during the Christmas holiday, my mother took me to see my grandfather, James Henry Lewis, who, like his father A. L. Lewis, did not have much formal education but worked in the family's insurance business. Through hard work, he eventually rose to a top leadership position and became a wealthy and prominent citizen of Jacksonville.

My mother left the room where Papa, as I called my grandfather, and I sat to talk. The first thing my grandfather asked me was: "So, baby girl, when are you going to start working in the family's insurance business?" I responded enthusiastically: "Papa, I am not going to work in the family's business, I'm going to become an anthropologist!" My grandfather's response was "What's that?" To which I said, "Oh Papa, I'm going to be like Margaret Mead and travel to different places in the world to learn about and teach about and write about how other people live." Papa quickly asked: "Baby Girl, how in the world are you going to make a living doing that?"

I was shocked and hurt by my grandfather's response, but I put my emotions in check until Papa brought closure to our conversation, and I could run to find my mother. With tears streaming down my face, I told my mother what Papa had said to me and confessed that I was deeply hurt by his response to my determination to become an anthropologist.

My mother said to me: "First of all, your grandfather asked you a very important question because a young woman should have a plan for how she will not be dependent on the financial resources of her husband and figure out how she will be able to support herself." And then she said: "However, my daughter, if anthropology is your passion, then you must follow it!"

My mother would not have described herself as a Black feminist, but in so many ways she was. As I grew into being a Black feminist, not only in terms of how I entered the fields of anthropology, Black studies, and African American studies, I continuously reflected on how I had witnessed my mother living her life as what some would call a womanist, and others would say was a feminist.

As one would say in the world of art, my mother "had the eye."

As I have shared, my mother was an English major in college, and for several years, she taught English at the historically Black college in our hometown which is now Edward Waters University. My mother was also an accomplished pianist, organist, and director of all of the choirs at Mt Olive A.M.E Church where members of my family worshipped. And while she was not trained in the visual arts, and never worked in a museum, in the world of the visual arts she would be described in this way: "She has the eye!"

My mother adorned our homes with quality reproductions of the works of great artists, especially African American artists. And in our living room, there were art catalogs. They were too big for me to hold when I was a child, but I loved to kneel at the edge of the coffee table and turn the pages of those books that were filled with what I would come to understand many years later, were visual stories of the lives of various peoples in the world.

As I think about how I came to fall in love with the visual arts, especially the visual arts of Africa and the African diaspora, and how I came to serve as the Director of the Smithsonian National Museum of African Art, there is a line that can be traced directly back to my mother.

I am clearly my mother's child.

In each of the stories that I have told about my mother, it is so clear that she not only gave birth to me, but along with my Daddy, my family, and my community, she raised me. My mother was also the individual who had the strongest influence on who I have become. As a well-known saying puts it: "Apple don't fall far from the tree." I am eternally grateful to my mother for being the tree from which I have fallen.

Dr. Johnnetta Betsch Cole
Historic American Beach, Fernandina Beach, FL

Dr. Johnnetta Betsch Cole
(Photo courtesy of Dr. Johnnetta Cole)

Johnnetta Betsch Cole, Ph.D. is a noted anthropologist, educator, author, speaker, and consultant on inclusion, diversity, equity, and accessibility in educational institutions, museums, corporations, and other workplaces. After receiving a Ph.D. in anthropology, Dr. Cole held teaching positions in anthropology, women's studies, and African American studies at several colleges and universities. She was recently appointed a Kettering Foundation Senior fellow.

Dr. Cole served as President of both historically Black colleges for women in the United States, Spelman College and Bennett College, a distinction she alone holds. She also served as the Director of the Smithsonian National Museum of African Art, as a Principal Consultant at Cook Ross, and as a Senior Consulting Fellow at the Mellon Foundation.

Continuing her long involvement in community service, in 2004 Cole was the first African American to serve as the Chair of the Board of United Way of America. She recently served in the voluntary position of Chair of the Board and Seventh President of the National Council of Negro Women. Currently, she serves on the board of the A. L. Lewis Museum on Historic American Beach in Fernandina Beach, FL.

Dr. Cole has served on the corporate boards of Coca-Cola Enterprises, Home Depot, Merck, and Nation's Bank South. She was the first woman appointed to the board of Coca-Cola Enterprises and the first Black woman appointed to Merck's board of directors.

Johnnetta Betsch Cole has authored, co-authored, and edited several books and numerous articles for scholarly and general audiences. Her latest publications are *Speechifying: The Words and Legacy of Johnnetta Betsch Cole* (2023), *Racism in American Public Life: A Call to Action* (2021), and *African Proverbs for All Ages* (2021). Dr. Cole has received numerous awards and is the recipient of seventy honorary degrees. On March 21, 2023, Dr. Cole was awarded a National Humanities Medal by President Joseph Biden.

Throughout her career and in her published work, speeches, and community service, Johnnetta Betsch Cole consistently addresses issues of racism, sexism, and all other systems of inequality. She is a mentor to people of different identities and cultures. Dr. Cole is listed in *TheHistoryMakers.*

Melvia Wallace and her mother, Mrs. Linda Wallace

(Photo courtesy of Dr. Melvia Wallace)

"Mom taught all four of us to read by the age of three."

— Dr. Melvia Lynn Wallace

Mrs. Linda Mott Wallace

Written by Dr. Melvia Lynn Wallace / Daughter

When thinking about my relationship with my mother, I'd often say, "It's complicated." Until recently, it seemed that my mom and I had been at odds ever since she pushed me out of her womb. We are incredibly different. She is a Southern Belle (in my view), the youngest of nine children who were raised in Little Rock, AR.

Appearance is important to her. You'll never see my mom with even one hair out of place or without full makeup, even if she's just running to the store to pick up the one item that she forgot for her famous macaroni and cheese. It has only been in the past few years that she has given up her four-inch heels and her "foundations." At her tallest, she was about 5'2". She's "light-skinned" (her maternal grandmother was Irish), and when she married at age nineteen, her wedding dress was a size three.

I am the exact physical opposite of my mom. I'm darker skinned, I can't recall ever being smaller than a size ten (that was in my teens), and I prefer exercise pants, a sweatshirt, and a great pair of walking shoes to suits and heels. Growing up, I was a "daddy's girl." I was named after him, and I looked just like him when I was younger. While my mom constantly chided me about my weight and my appearance, my father told me that I didn't have to comb my hair and I believed that he loved me just the way I was. I felt as if I could never live up to my mother's physical expectations of me so, early on, I stopped trying.

My mother was raised in a strict household. Her father believed in the "spare the rod, spoil the child" philosophy. Mom adopted that tradition (mostly for me) and mostly because of my mouth. I am the oldest, was quite rebellious, and "talked back" a lot growing up. I was intent on doing things my way thus fueling many arguments with my mom. This resulted in a lot of spankings for me. I thought my mother was mean and I frequently told her that she wasn't "fair." Mom wasn't the hugging type, and she gave very few compliments. Quite frankly, I didn't think my mother liked me.

Mrs. Linda Wallace and her young daughters, Melvia and Monica (in arms)
(Photo courtesy of Melvia Wallace)

When I answered the call from Paulette to write about how my mother inspired me, I had to admit that I'd never really given it much thought. However, as I began to reflect on my life, I realized just how much I had learned from my mother, and how those lessons have carried me through the darkest and most challenging moments of my life.

My mom taught me excellence. She used to say, "Whatever you do, do it well and do it right the first time." I always have. I remember perfecting my penmanship in elementary school. My homework was always impeccably written. Excellence has been so much a part of my success that it is now one of my company's operating principles.

My mom taught me the love and support of family. Mom will do anything for her family, and she will defend her children and grandchildren to the death. When we were growing up, we all knew that the one sure way to get a spanking was to fight with our siblings. If we were fighting like cats and dogs after Mom left the house, we quickly squashed it when we heard her car enter the garage. No amount of harm that we did to each other could compare to the spanking we would get from my mom for fighting. "You don't fight with your siblings." Period.

My mom values education. This was an early and consistent message from both parents. Mom taught all four of us to read by the age of three. When I was in the fifth grade, my teacher sent me to classes with sixth graders because I had mastered all the fifth-grade work. My teacher eventually wrote to my parents to get their permission for me to skip the sixth grade. I was upset at this prospect because I had just been elected captain of the patrols for the coming year. My parents ignored my resistance, and in the fall, I entered junior high school.

Mrs. Linda Wallace and her children and grandchildren
Top: Melvia, Serena, Shelby, Monica
Middle: Brandi, Ariana, Isaiah,
Lower: Austin, Mrs. Wallace, Douglas
Christian (bottom left)
(Photo courtesy of Melvia Wallace)

When I was in the ninth grade, the teacher and sponsor for the National Junior Honor Society (NJHS) told me that I would not be inducted even though I had met all the criteria of scholarship, service, leadership, character, and citizenship. I was recognized as one of the smartest students in the entire school. I had a straight "A" average, held leadership positions in various clubs and organizations, and was very involved in community activities. There was just one problem, I wasn't the right color. Upon hearing this news, both my parents took off work and marched into the principal's office to meet with him and the NJHS sponsor. They wanted to hear the reasoning for why I was being denied entry. As a result of that meeting, I was inducted into NJHS later that semester, along with my classmates.

Growing up, it was an unspoken expectation that all four of my parents' children would attend college.

While we had the freedom to choose where we would go, we did not have the choice not to go. As a result, my parents have four college-educated children with nine degrees among them—quite an accomplishment.

My mom taught me courage and resilience. No matter what happened in her life, Mom had a way of picking herself up, dusting herself off, and starting over again. I saw that best in 2017 when she was diagnosed with breast cancer and, in the thick of her treatments and the trauma of hair loss, her oldest grandson, my beloved nephew, Austin, passed away. It was the first time that I could recall seeing my mom cry. She raised Austin in his early years while my sister completed medical school. She and Austin had an unbreakable bond. The weight of cancer treatments and the loss of her beloved Austin was just too much to bear. I am certain it was the lowest point in her life, but she fought through it.

I witnessed this same courage and resilience over this past year as I watched my mom care for my dad during his final year of life. As I reflect, I realize that she has spent her entire adult life with my dad, so this was probably the most difficult year of her life. My dad was a full foot taller than my mother and about fifty pounds heavier, but she bathed and fed and groomed and changed bandages and cleaned his clothes and brushed his teeth and read to him and loved him until he took his last breath on February 21, 2023. This dedicated care was also a reflection of her loyalty. Regardless of the ups and downs of their nearly sixty-year marriage, she took her vows, "till death do us part," very seriously. My mom has lifelong friends, some she's known for nearly seventy years. She has been a loyal and caring friend to them also.

Finally, and most importantly, my mother is guided by her faith in God. We grew up in church. For several years, while my mom was the church secretary, we were in church school and choir rehearsal all day on Saturdays. We were also in church practically every Sunday morning. I have lifelong friends from those early years at church. It was my grounding. My mom isn't preachy in her faith, yet she has a fundamental belief that things will work themselves out. I will never forget several years ago when I was going through a rough patch in my life, she told me to "take it to God and leave it there." I took Mom's advice, and it was the best advice that I've ever gotten from her. It has never failed me.

Melvin and Linda Wallace
(Photo courtesy of Melvia Wallace)

So, in writing this, as I reflect on my relationship with my mother, I realize that I have grown to understand her. Our relationship has transitioned into a wonderful friendship. I dress up more. We've both softened up a bit. And we share a common grief: the loss of a spouse. Our relationship isn't that complicated after all. It's actually very simple. Everything that I am (educated, a woman of faith, caring, strong, loyal, family-oriented, courageous, resilient, and reliable) and everything I have accomplished is because of my mother.

I love you, Mom!

Melvia Wallace, Ed.D.
Upper Marlboro, Maryland

Dr. Melvia Lynn Wallace
(Photo courtesy of Dr. Wallace)

Dr. Melvia Lynn Wallace spent her early career at Xerox Corporation and Procter & Gamble Company holding positions in Finance, Organizational Development, Total Quality Management, Manufacturing, and Global Supply Chain Management.

Dr. Wallace has provided professional training and development at the corporate level. Her clients included Procter & Gamble, AT&T, and Educational Testing Service.

In 2001, Melvia and her late husband, Jerry, co-founded The Austin Group, LLC (TAG), a management consulting firm, where she currently serves as CEO. Their clients include hospitals, mental health and drug rehabilitation agencies, youth rehabilitation service agencies, community colleges and universities, public housing authorities, workforce development companies, and local, state, and federal government agencies.

In 2006, Melvia and Jerry established The Family Health and Education Institute (FHEI). FHEI, is a non-profit organization that served hundreds of fathers by providing critical life skills, employment preparation, and job training that allowed them to attain livable wages to support their families. Their *Inner Journey Training*® model was identified as a "promising practice" by the U.S. Department of Health and Human Services. Out of this work, she and Jerry co-authored *Turning the Corner - Strategies for Helping Urban Males Navigate the Pathway to Success*.

Dr. Wallace has volunteered extensively for her *alma mater*, Duke University. She has served in various leadership roles including President of the Duke University Black Alumni Connection and as a member of the Board of Directors of the Duke University Alumni Association. As a result of her service, Dr. Wallace was awarded both the Forever Duke Award for Excellence in Volunteer Service and the Charles A. Dukes Award for Extraordinary Long-term Volunteer Leadership.

Dr. Wallace received a Bachelor of Science degree in Computer Science and Psychology from Duke University, a master's in business administration from Clark Atlanta University, and a Doctorate in Education from Rutgers University.

Dr. Wallace is a proud member of Delta Sigma Theta Sorority, Inc. She is currently engaging in her "second act" as a voice-over artist! She resides in Upper Marlboro, Maryland.

Mrs. Kittie Mathis

(Photo courtesy of Janice Mathis)

"Mama continually encouraged us to learn. She had one basic prescription for every condition. If you were in a bad mood, she would say, 'Why don't you read a book?' If you misbehaved, it was 'You should go to your room and read a book.' If you were good the reward was 'You deserve a new book.'"

— Janice L. Mathis, Esq.

HONORING

Mrs. Kittie Avery Mathis

Written by Janice L. Mathis, Esq. / Daughter

Mama, Mrs. Kittie Avery Mathis, was civic-minded. She always voted. The neighborhood polling place was conveniently located a block from the house. My sister and I walked with her to vote. We were entranced by the curtain-draped polling booths, the paper ballots, and the mystery of it all. I don't recall any candidate she voted for except John F. Kennedy for president. She voted for President Kennedy despite Daddy's protestant protestations about the possible influence of the papacy on the presidency.

Mama was also independent. She did not hesitate to speak her mind to Daddy or us, but generally in a measured thoughtful way. She said, "I don't see why I should have to spank you; you have above-average intelligence. I should be able to reason with you." When he was called into the ministry after fifteen years of marriage, Mama organized her life around Vacation Bible School, and Christmas and Easter pageants.

Mama continually encouraged us to learn. She had one basic prescription for every condition. If you were in a bad mood, she would say, "Why don't you read a book?" If you misbehaved, it was "You should go to your room and read a book." If you were good the reward was "You deserve a new book." Over the years I realized that reading was the point. Learning continued through the summer, in day camp, at Christ Episcopal Church, and Bennett College.

Mama's real superpower was skillful inquisition. In my forty-plus years of practicing law, I have not met anyone with better cross-examination skills or a better understanding of the Socratic method. After a date, she would ask, "How was the movie?" or "Who was in the film?" I knew that she was making sure we went where we said we were going. A few times when I was peering into the mirror, she would ask, "Do you like what you see?" She never waited for an answer, she just let you sit with the question. I came to understand from her inquiry that my opinion of me mattered more than any other.

Mama loved movies and magazines, fashion, dancing, and food. Bridge Club and missionary society meetings at the house were affairs not to be missed. She studied cookbooks and magazines to devise a perfectly executed menu of special occasion treats. She made draperies, slipcovers, coats, and suits. No tailoring project was beyond her skill set. The more intricate the pattern, the more she seemed to enjoy it. Mama was the youngest of five siblings and the only one who did not move in the Great Migration from South

Carolina to New York. It was her siblings war industry salaries that funded her degree in tailoring from North Carolina A&T.

The Mathis Family
Joseph, Kittie, Davida, and Janice
(Photo courtesy of Janice Mathis)

My parents did not always agree. Sometimes they clashed over parenting. She wanted obedience, while Daddy was more inclined toward raising independent thinkers. More than once he was heard to say, "How will they learn to make decisions if you decide everything for them?" Her reply was something like, "I don't have time for them to make decisions today. I need them to get dressed." He loved to spend; she loved to save. She actually read the investment prospectus for fun.

My mother gave me the timeless gifts of faith, curiosity, frugality, generosity, and appreciation of art in all its forms. I still don't know how the daughter of a Pullman porter and a laundress developed into an artistic, compassionate, generous, and devoted mother, but every day I am grateful that she did.

Janice L. Mathis, Esq.
Washington, D.C.

Janice Mathis, Esq.
(Photo courtesy of Janice Mathis)

Janice L. Mathis, Esq. was appointed General Council of the National Council of Negro Women (NCNW) in 2023 when she transitioned from the position of Executive Director which she held since 2016. NCNW's mission is to lead, advocate for, and empower women of African descent, their families, and communities. Under her leadership, NCNW's program and social justice agendas were expanded significantly to include entrepreneurship, health equity, voting rights, ending violence against women, and student loan debt reduction.

Before joining NCNW, Janice was General Counsel and Vice President of Rev. Jesse L. Jackson's Rainbow PUSH Coalition and the Citizenship Education Fund. She spearheaded civil rights and diversity initiatives and led the successful Keep the Vote Alive campaign in 2005 to reauthorize the Voting Rights Act.

Janice practiced real estate, bankruptcy, probate, and personal injury law for nearly two decades in a firm she started with several law school classmates. She was appointed Special Assistant Attorney General for the State of Georgia, representing Child Support Enforcement and the Georgia Department of Transportation. She served as a speechwriter and Deputy Issues Director for Michael S. Dukakis' 1988 presidential campaign.

In recent years, Janice helped to found Power Rising, a national networking group of African American women. She also founded the Metro Athens Growth Federation to spur job creation in Athens, GA. As President of the Morton Theatre Corporation, she revived a turn-of-the-20th-century office and entertainment complex in Athen's that was originally built by Pink Morton, a Black entrepreneur. She testified before the United Nations Commission in Switzerland to End Racial Discrimination.

Ms. Mathis has been honored by numerous organizations, including Delta Sigma Theta Sorority, Atlanta Business League, Rolling Out Magazine, Good Housekeeping, and the 1996 Centennial Olympics.

Janice earned Bachelor of Arts degrees in economics and public policy studies at Duke University and is a graduate of the Lumpkin School of Law at the University of Georgia in Athens.

Janice served on numerous boards including the Athens Area Community Foundation, United Way of Northeast Georgia, Athens Area OIC, and Delta Sigma Theta Sorority's National Social Action Commission. Janice formerly served as a member of the Rules Committee of the Democratic National Committee and on the national board of the League of Women Voters of the U.S.

Janice is widowed and is a "bonus mom" to two adult children raised in her home and "GranJan" to three beautiful grandchildren who are the light of her life.

Mrs. Lillian Dunn Perry

(Photo courtesy of Beatrice Soublet)

*"You had discounted the power
of a mother's prayer."*

— Beatrice Perry Soublet

HONORING

Mrs. Lillian Dunn Perry

Written by Beatrice Perry Soublet / Daughter

My mother, Lillian Dunn Perry, always used her maiden name as her middle name. Perhaps it was because her father, a prominent minister and social activist, had five daughters and no son to carry on his name. She was an extremely talented musician who used her gifts as a music teacher, accompanist, choir director, and minister of music. She made certain that I developed my gifts by participating in culturally uplifting activities and organizations.

My mother did not allow herself to be diminished by the insulting laws of Jim Crow. One day when we were shopping in Maison Blanche, a popular department store in New Orleans, the salesperson was intent on waiting on every White person in the line no matter when they arrived. In her teacher's voice and volume, my mother called this to her attention "My daughter and I were here first." We were quickly served.

Mom valued keeping her commitments and standing by her word, a lesson she taught me when I was a senior in high school. It was the responsibility of every chorus student who could play the piano to accompany the chorus for a semester. Unfortunately, my turn fell during the Christmas season. I had to play the "Hallelujah" chorus from Handel's Messiah. I told my mom that there were too many notes, and it was too hard, so I couldn't do it. She reminded me that I had given my word. She practiced with me, focusing on the exposed parts and the base. Fortunately, I made it through, and so did the chorus.

When my mother left New Orleans to go to graduate school in New York, (education was highly valued by our family) she arranged for me to live with my grandmother for a year rather than stay at home with my father and my brother. While my grandmother's house was only a few blocks away, being away from my father and my brother seemed like a world away. Regardless of my protests, she knew what was best for me and did it.

My mother had an unwavering faith which she exemplified through her belief in the efficacy of prayer. When I was four years old, I had spinal meningitis. The doctors told my mother that I probably would not live. When I recovered, my mother said to them, "You discounted the power of a mother's prayer." Her faith compelled her to ensure that I attended Sunday school, received my First Communion and Confirmation, and participated in the church youth group.

Mrs. Lillian Perry and her daughter, Beatrice Soublet
(Photo courtesy of Beatrice Soublet)

Sometimes, children are not aware of the sacrifices that are made for them by their parents. I however, remember very well one instance in which my mom made a very obvious sacrifice for me. When I headed off to college, my mother, who certainly could have used a new coat, bought me a lovely black file coat with a silver mink collar. I only saw the beauty of the coat and, of course, not the underlying sacrifice that made it possible.

So, what did I learn from this dear lady, whom I nicknamed "Diamond Lil", because of her love for those gems and her diamond-like qualities? She sparkled, she was strong, and she was genuine. I learned to provide valuable activities and involvements for my children. I learned to teach my children to stand up against a system that would attempt to diminish them. I also taught my children that their word is their bond. I involved them in church and other activities that built character. I taught them the value of education. I helped them learn the gift of being generous and kind. All of this is the legacy of my mother's training and guidance.

Beatrice Perry Soublet
Atlanta, GA

Beatrice Perry Soublet, a native of New Orleans, LA, is a poet and educator who migrated to Atlanta, GA after Hurricane Katrina. She currently resides in East Point, GA. Beatrice retired as principal of St. Mary of the Angels Catholic School in New Orleans.

A poet and retired educator, "Ms. Bea," as she is fondly called, has authored several books of poetry including *Watchwords: Thoughts on Race, Water, and War* and *Always Bring Your Sunglasses*, both of which are available on Amazon. Her artistic excellence has been recognized by her sorority, Delta Sigma Theta Sorority, Inc., with the Literary Arts Award in 1985 and 1998, and by the Amistad Research Center. She was recently commissioned by her faith community, the historic Our Lady of Lourdes Catholic Church in Atlanta, to write a poem commemorating its 110th anniversary.

Ms. Bea participated in the 1962 sit-ins in Greensboro, NC, and was arrested at the South African Embassy in Washington, D.C. for her protest of the evil system of Apartheid. She has been recognized locally and nationally as a committed and effective advocate for issues related to social justice and racial equity. In 2009, Bea received the Social Justice Award from Church Women United and the Father Bruce Wilkerson Founder's Award in 2012. She, and her late husband, Lawrence C. Soublet, Jr., co-founded the Atlanta branch of ERACE, a racial discussion group. She currently co-chairs the Our Lady of Lourdes Catholic Church's Social Justice Committee and remains active in several social justice advocacy initiatives. She also advocates for children's issues with the Interfaith Children's Movement. Bea volunteers at her church to provide food, clothing, and other services for the unhoused population in the historic Old Fourth Ward of Atlanta.

Beatrice is a graduate of Bennett College and The George Washington University. She is an active member of Delta Sigma Theta, Inc., the NAACP, and is a member of the Wendel Whalem Community Choir in Atlanta for which she has served as president. She is the mother of a son, the late Nathaniel T. Stanley, and a daughter, Kathryn V. Stanley.

"The true worth of a race must be measured by the character of its womanhood."

Dr. Mary McLeod Bethune

"I am my mother's daughter and the drums of Africa still beat in my heart."

Dr. Mary McLeod Bethune

Paulette Lewis and her mother, Velma Norvel

When You Thought I Wasn't Looking

by Mary Rita Schilke Sill

When you thought I wasn't looking
You hung my first painting on the refrigerator
And I wanted to paint another.

When you thought I wasn't looking
You fed a stray cat
And I thought it was good to be kind to animals.

When you thought I wasn't looking
You baked a birthday cake just for me
And I knew that little things were special things.

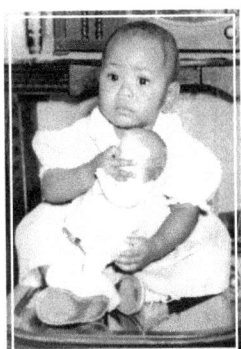

Paulette Norvel Lewis

When you thought I wasn't looking
You said a prayer
And I believed there was a God that I could always talk to.

When you thought I wasn't looking
You kissed me goodnight
And I felt loved.

When you thought I wasn't looking
I saw tears come from your eyes
And I learned that sometimes things hurt
But that it's all right to cry.

When you thought I wasn't looking
You smiled and it made me want to look that pretty too.

When you thought I wasn't looking
You cared
And I wanted to be everything I could be.

When you thought I wasn't looking
I looked
And I wanted to say thanks
For all the things you did
When you thought I wasn't looking.

"We delight in the beauty of the butterfly, but we rarely admit the changes it has gone through to achieve that beauty."

Maya Angelou

Mrs. Gloria Broadus Caponis and daughter, Alexis Herman

(Photo courtesy of Alexis Herman)

*"Acting in the presence of fear was
her definition of courage."*

— Alexis Herman

HONORING

Mrs. Gloria Broadus Caponis

Written by Alexis Herman / Daughter

My mother, Gloria Broadus Caponis, was a single mom who dedicated her life to taking care of me. After all these years, I recognize a powerful truth that was not evident to me during my formative years. Simply put, our lives are shaped by the choices we make, whether good or bad. Owning these choices and taking responsibility for them is not something we always do well. My mother owned her choices, and I never heard her complain or make excuses for what was both a painful and joyful life.

Mrs. Gloria Broadus Caponis
(Photo courtesy of Alexis Herman)

Momie chose to bring me into this world at the age of twenty. She returned to college when I was three to earn a degree in education. We pursued master's degrees together while she was in her forties. My mother never allowed the biases of the time against single moms to limit her choices in life.

My mother pursued a spirit of excellence. While in her fifties, she was the first African American to be named Alabama Reading Teacher of the Year. Throughout her teaching career, she tutored children in our home and on weekends, after school, and summers, especially those with reading disabilities. My mother poured herself into me and her work. I was always included, and I never felt disconnected from her as I assisted with the children who were everywhere in our home. That same spirit of excellence was instilled in me early on, in whatever tasks I was called to perform. She modeled a "can do" attitude and service, no matter the odds, especially with her students and me.

I was reminded of this at my mother's funeral when a former student, who is now a high school principal, gave his testimony about her. At age fourteen, he still could not read. My mother asked him what he wanted to do more than anything else in life. He said he wanted to learn to drive a car. Momie drove him to the Mobile Motor Vehicle Bureau and together they picked up all the driving manuals. Using these manuals, she proceeded to teach him to read so that he could achieve his dream of learning to drive and securing a driver's license. She always said there was no such thing as a dumb child. Only a child you hadn't found a way to reach.

Mrs. Caponis, her daughter, Alexis, and Paulette Norvel
(Photo courtesy of Alexis Herman)

Acting in the presence of fear was my mother's definition of courage. When I was six or seven, we were walking home from downtown Mobile after a hard day of work for my mother. Tired and weary, she decided about halfway home that we would take the bus the rest of the way. We boarded the bus and she literally collapsed on the front seat. The bus driver immediately stopped the bus and said, "Lady, you can't sit there." When she refused to move, either from exhaustion or maybe that was just the day she had had enough, the bus driver pulled her off her seat, opened the front door, and pushed her onto the street. With tears in her eyes, torn stockings, and struggling to get off her knees, she held her head high and said to me, "Come on Alexis, we will just keep walking." She just kept moving. At critical times throughout my life, that life lesson has been my special mantra, "keep it moving." Whenever I encounter difficulties and want to shut down, especially when facing injustices, I work at keeping my head high and focusing on the solution rather than the problem. I keep it moving.

Our home was always a welcoming center full of love, family, and friends. It was that welcoming spirit that enabled a thirteen-year-old girl, whom we had never met, to come live with us in our two-bedroom house. That young girl was not permitted to attend the White Catholic high school less than a mile from her home in Pascagoula, MS. Instead, she had to choose the nearest Black Catholic school in Mobile, AL. When my mother heard the story of her family's dilemma from a friend, she decided it was time for me to share my bedroom with the sister I always wanted. That young girl is the author of this book, and my sister to this day, Paulette Lewis. My mother understood the joy of giving and being there for others, especially in times of need.

Dr. F. Ray Marshall, U.S. Secretary of Labor,
Alexis Herman, Director of the Women's Bureau (center)
And her mother, Mrs. Caponis, holding the Bible
for her daughter's swearing-in ceremony
(Photo courtesy of Alexis Herman)

While my mother had great strength and opened doors for others, she also had periods of pain and disappointment and even brief periods of depression. She shared her vulnerability and allowed me to experience those moments with her, whether it was shedding tears over unpaid bills or her unfulfilled desire for a husband who met her aspirational picture of love. She married briefly and later divorced an abusive man when I was ten or eleven. Her lifelong desire for a loving and kind husband helped me to define what was important in a marriage, trust, fidelity, and shared values.

Momie's faith was a source of strength through all of life's challenges. As a Catholic, I did not attend Bible study or Sunday school growing up, so I was not a student of the Bible. My mother became a student of the Bible as she grew older. When I was twenty-nine, I was appointed the youngest-ever Director of the Women's Bureau in the U.S. Department of Labor by President Carter. My mother gave me my first Bible for the swearing-in. She inscribed it with the words from Proverbs 3, "Lean not on your own understanding but acknowledge Him in all of your ways and He will direct your path." These words were probably the most precious gift she left me with when she passed away at the young age of sixty-four. I am now a student of the Bible and the Bible that she gave to me is one of my most treasured possessions. I have used it for subsequent swearing-in ceremonies, and it is featured in my official photo as the U.S. Secretary of Labor.

We will not always have the answer to all our challenges. Life can and does often defy human reasoning. But a spirit of acceptance, patience, and hope can bring peace to one's soul. Acknowledging this reality and coming to understand my mother's perfections and imperfections, has helped to make me who I am today.

Dr. Dorothy Irene Height, Past President of the National Council of Negro Women, Inc. and her surrogate daughter, Alexis Herman, at the 2008 Democratic National Convention
(Photo by and courtesy of Paulette Norvel Lewis)

In addition to my mother, I was blessed to have had Dorothy Height, President of the National Council of Negro Women, as my surrogate mother for more than forty years. She knew my mother and loved her gumbo at Christmastime. It was Dr. Height who continued to inspire and support me especially when I was named Secretary of Labor. Dr. Height was a recipient of the Congressional Gold Medal. The words inscribed on that medal, "We as African American women don't always get to do what we want to do, but we always do what we have to do." epitomized Momie's life. She probably would have added, "Keep it moving." I am eternally grateful for their guidance and inspiring example of courage, service, and love.

The Honorable Alexis Herman
McLean, VA

The Honorable Alexis Herman
(Photo courtesy of Paulette Norvel Lewis)

The Honorable Alexis M. Herman was born in Mobile, AL. She began her career working for Catholic Charities helping young out-of-school men and women find work in the Pascagoula, MS shipyard. In addition to pioneering apprenticeship opportunities for these youth, she also led efforts to place the first women of color into professional and technical positions in major corporations including General Motors, Delta Airlines, and Coca-Cola. These efforts led her to the appointment at age twenty-nine, by President Jimmy Carter, to be the youngest Director of the Women's Bureau in the history of the Labor Department. In 1992, she became the first African American woman to serve as an Assistant to the President and the Director of the White House Office of Public Liaison, in the Clinton Administration. On May 1, 1997, Alexis M. Herman was sworn in as America's twenty-third Secretary of Labor and the first African American ever to lead the United States Department of Labor. During her tenure as a member of the president's cabinet, she also served as a valued member of the National Economic Council.

As Secretary, she focused on a prepared workforce, a secure workforce, and quality workplaces. She led the effort to institute a global child labor standard, moved people from welfare to work with dignity, and launched the most aggressive unemployed youth initiative since the 1970s. Under her tenure, unemployment in the country reached a thirty-year low and witnessed the safest workplace record in the history of the Department of Labor. Alexis Herman's actions as Secretary reflected her understanding of the needs of America's workers and the challenges they faced as this nation approached the 21st Century.

Her Father served as the first African American elected to any political office in the deep South in the 1940s. He instilled in her a belief in the political process to create meaningful change. From her teenage years of working for voter registration to serving as Chief of Staff, Deputy Chair of the Democratic National

Committee, and Co-Chair of the Price-Herman Commission on Presidential Primaries, Ms. Herman has always remained committed to helping others secure their political and economic rights.

Upon leaving government service, Ms. Herman chose the entrepreneurial career path. This path was inspired by her efforts to establish the first federal government policy to assist women business owners in the Carter Administration. Currently, Ms. Herman serves as chair and chief executive officer of New Ventures, LLC, a Risk Management Firm. She has continued to lend her expertise and talent to a vast array of corporate enterprises and nonprofit organizations. The recipient of numerous awards and honors, she has received more than thirty honorary doctorate degrees from major colleges and universities. She is also an inductee in the Minority Business Hall of Fame, the National Women's History Project, *TheHistoryMakers*, and the first African American woman inducted into the Alabama Business Hall of Fame in 2022. Ms. Herman is a former trustee for the establishment of the Martin Luther King Jr. Memorial, a former trustee of her alma mater, Xavier University of Louisiana, and is currently a trustee of the Toyota Technological Institute at Chicago University. She co-chaired the Bush-Clinton Katrina Fund and is presently Co-Chair of the Bush-Clinton Presidential Leadership Scholars. Ms. Herman served as the former Lead Director of Cummins Inc., and a member of the board of directors of Entergy. Presently, she is a member of MGM Resorts International and The Coca-Cola Company board of directors. Additionally, she chairs the Diversity Advisory Board for The Toyota Motor Company. In her public service, as well as her non-profit work, Ms. Herman has served five Presidents of the United States, both Democrat and Republican. Her nonprofit work today includes being a Trustee for the National Urban League, Honorary Chair of the Social Action Committee, for her sorority, Delta Sigma Theta, Inc., and President of the Dorothy I. Height Education Foundation.

Ms. DeAnna Lewis and
her daughter, Nina Lange

(Photo courtesy of Nina Lange)

"My mother, on the other hand, knew that I did not
need their help, advice, or grounding. I needed support
and reassurance, and she always provided that."

— Nina Rose Lange

HONORING

HONORING

Ms. DeAnna Marie Lewis

Written by Nina Rose Lange / Daughter

Nina Lange and her mom, Ms. DeAnna Lewis
(Photo courtesy of Nina Lange)

I have never felt that I looked like my mother. My eyes, my nose, my hair, and the shape of my face are all different from hers. I have never looked at any of my photographs and seen my mother or gazed into a mirror and felt like she was staring back at me. When I was younger, I imagined that I was secretly adopted or somehow switched at birth.

My mother, DeAnna Marie Lewis, is and always will be very extroverted. Everyone who has ever met me immediately perceives me as standoffish and quiet. Looking at my mother and me, you would never guess that we are related. But she has always understood that we are really very much alike, despite our appearances and inferred personalities. She knew that I was more of an "internal extrovert" rather than an obvious extrovert like her. Internally, I am adventurous, curious, and even daring. When these characteristics are exposed, they come as a surprise to everyone except my mother.

Unlike many mothers, my mom always encouraged me to go to parties and concerts, have fun, and "live life to the fullest." She trusted me and knew that I was responsible enough to handle myself. In the past, I have had rather lofty goals and even outrageous plans that many people have criticized in an effort to "bring me back down to earth," to what they considered "reality." In their own way, they were concerned and tried to help me. My mother, on the other hand, knew that I did not need their help, advice, or grounding. I needed support and reassurance, and she always provided that.

Nina Lange and her mother, Ms. DeAnna Lewis
(Photo courtesy of Nina Lange)

Without my mother, I would never have found the confidence to live out my dreams. When I think of our relationship so far, our car, the 2007 Honda Accord, was a focal point. I recently named her "Chelsey." Chelsey has been with us through thick and thin and all the stages of my growth and development. As I sat in my booster seat in the back of Chelsey, I wondered how my mother knew the directions to everywhere we needed to go. When we brought a stray cat home (though I still don't understand how she allowed me to do that), we rode home in Chelsey. After a long day of elementary school, I would throw my backpack in and begin to tell my mother about the kids who irritated me in class. In middle school, I had my notorious "car apple" each day, and she never questioned my strangeness.

Though it was a stressful ordeal, my mother taught me to drive in Chelsey, helping me to overcome one of my greatest fears. And as I grew older, Chelsey became the treasured place where we spent most of our quality time. With no other distractions or preoccupations, no deadlines or business meetings, late nights and long drives in Chelsey became our bonding time. It was there that I learned things about my mother's past, her viewpoints, and her dreams, and we talked like old friends. With every word she said, I learned life lessons and made memories. I formed an image in my mind of who she was before I existed, and it fascinated me.

Mom and I also share and enjoy music, cooking, and decorating together for our annual Mardi Gras and Halloween parties, going to concerts, and road trips. She's a huge Dave Matthews fan and enjoys going to his concerts as often as she can. I introduced her to Bon Iver and we go to those concerts together.

I now reflect on the countless sacrifices that my mom has made as a single mother. From the moment I was born, her life was irreversibly changed. The car itself is a great example of this reality. Though she always longed for a vehicle with high speed and performance, she opted for the practical, child-friendly, and unremarkable Accord. Not only that, but she also kept this car through its countless breakdowns, repairs, and accidents, and all 375,000 miles. She put me through private school and sent me to my favorite summer camps. She moved across town so that I could attend a more highly-regarded high school where I could have better opportunities and a better education. She flew with me to Italy to tour the university that I had been talking about for years. I have heard many parents tell their children how much worse their lives were when they were young and that their children should be grateful for whatever they had, no matter how small. My mother never did this to me. No matter what struggles she may have had in her youth, getting an education, pursuing her career, or in her personal life, she has always done everything in her power to ensure that I could have a better life, full of opportunities with room for growth and exploration. Though we still love and cherish Chelsey, I am happy to say that my mother has been able to get the car that she deserves, an all-black and very fast Mustang named Black Girl Magic, or Magic for short.

I imagine that being a mother must be extraordinarily difficult. I think as children we think of ourselves as different from our mothers. We expect them to know it all and get everything right on the first try. But as daughters, we inevitably grow older and realize that we are the same. We are all going through life for the first time and looking for someone to reach out to. I only hope that through the years I have been understanding and forgiving of her, because I could not have asked for a better mother. Through our differences, I think we bring out the good in each other and inspire one another to pursue the dreams that we need courage and encouragement to achieve. I am proud of her, and she is proud of me. Thinking of my mother makes me want to have a daughter of my own, so that maybe, even in my imperfection and my stubbornness, I can be for some little girl what my mother has been for me and provide the love and support that I had.

Nina Rose Lange
Rome, Italy

Nina Rose Lange
(Photos courtesy of Nina Lange)

Because of her mother's sacrifices, support, and encouragement, **Nina Rose Lange** is enjoying her first year of college at John Cabot University in Rome, Italy. After applying, Nina received a scholarship. Following the assessment of her high school transcript and a test, she was accepted as a sophomore rather than a freshman. She is studying communications with a minor in entrepreneurship.

Nina loves to travel, go to concerts, hike, build things, and do astrophotography. Some of her favorite pastimes are reading, writing, sewing, cooking, and most of all, listening to music. She hopes to someday own a flower shop or bookstore and eventually travel the world. The Vatican is visible from the front stoop of her apartment. She boasts that the Pope is her neighbor. Lucky man!

Mrs. Mable Wesley

(Photo courtesy of Beverly Thomas)

"Helping others was who she was!"

— Beverly Wesley Thomas

HONORING

Mrs. Mable Jeannette Wilson Wesley, MSW

Written by Beverly Wesley Thomas / Daughter

Mable Jeanette Wesley was born in Jackson, MS on April 18, 1917. She was the third of fourteen children born to Julia and Emmett Wilson. She was always the beloved matriarch of the Wilson clan. My mother could have aptly been named "Joy." She exuded joy from her heart and shared that joy through her smile, words of encouragement, and helping hand. Mom was not "preachy" however, when the opportunity presented itself, she let everyone know that God was the "center of her joy" and, that God was there for them also.

After graduating with her B.A. degree from Lincoln University, Mom met and married my father, Jacob Wesley. They had five children: Jacob Jr., Beverly, Jacqueline, Sherry, and Terry.

Beverly Thomas (standing), her mother, Mrs. Mable Wesley,
and sister, Michele Wesley
(Photo courtesy of Beverly Thomas)

In 1959, as the family was traveling to a family gathering in Jackson, MS, our station wagon was hit by a semi-truck. Four of my siblings, as well as my grandmother, were killed in the accident. My parents and I were the only survivors. Mom, Dad, and our entire family were completely devastated! Dad was the first to get out of hospital and he was the one who told me that my siblings had all perished in the accident. I stayed in the hospital from July to December where I "celebrated" my thirteenth birthday. I was released from the hospital in December, and we were finally able to travel back home to Los Angeles by train, accompanied by a nurse.

Mom and Dad's strong faith in God and the support of family and friends helped us to move from grief to gratitude. Years after losing their four children, Mom and Dad decided to adopt a baby girl, Michele, who brought much joy and happiness to the family.

Mom was a licensed social worker. Armed with her master's degree, she was passionately committed to that profession in the public school system of Los Angeles County for more than twenty-five years. Helping others was who she was!

Mrs. Beverly Thomas and her mother, Mrs. Mable Wesley
(Photo courtesy of Beverly Thomas)

When I think of my mother, many words come to mind:

Inspiration: Mom constantly encouraged and helped others. Her strength and abundant love for all encouraged and gave hope to all who knew her. There was not a judgmental bone in her body. In her mind, the question was never, "What's wrong with her?" but rather "What happened to her? What is she going through? How can I help?" She modeled that attitude and inspired others to extend the same compassion to others.

Encouragement: Mom always told me that I could do anything I wanted to in life. She encouraged me to continue moving forward and hold my head high no matter what situation I encountered. Her motto was always: "Put God first and keep on stepping."

Faith-based Strength: When I experienced challenges in life that seemed beyond my control, Mom was my strength. Her example and counsel always encouraged me to go on and not crumble. She taught me that God was always there for me and with me. She empowered me to reach within myself and realize that I must go forward not only for myself but also for my loved ones.

Helper: Mom and Dad were always there for family, friends, and others no matter what time of day or night. In her senior years, she regularly went outside in the afternoons to sit on a bench at the corner intersection of our home. This was her opportunity to get fresh air but more importantly, she knew that she could still be helpful to young adults as they navigated life. As neighbors in our subdivision returned from work, they often stopped to speak but also to get her encouragement and wise counsel regarding problems they were facing. She was a social worker to the end. Mom got joy from helping others and I have done the same throughout my life. It is so fulfilling to do for others and do it from the heart, expecting nothing in return.

Mom lived to one hundred and three years of age. Though she is with the Lord, I talk to her almost daily, and her spirit calms me. I can handle all situations just knowing she is listening. I ask myself "What would Mom do?" and then everything becomes clear.

I miss you so much, Mom!

Loving you forever,

Beverly Wesley Thomas
Los Angeles, CA

The Wesley Family
Beverly, the matriarch, in the middle
(Photo courtesy of Beverly Thomas)

Beverly Wesley Thomas (center) lives in Los Angeles, CA. Her life was forever changed and disrupted when at the age of thirteen, four of her siblings and her maternal grandmother were killed in an automobile accident as they were driving to Jackson, MS to vacation with family. Beverly and her parents were the only survivors. They were able to return home, accompanied by a nurse, after multiple surgeries and months in the hospital. Her parents subsequently adopted a daughter, Michele, who, with Beverly, brought great joy to their home.

Beverly attended Widney Handicapped School, graduated from Manual Arts High School, and attended Grambling College for two years. She worked for the Los Angeles Unified School District as an Office Manager for over twenty-five years. She retired to take care of her parents.

Beverly had two children, Nicole, and Terrence, (who passed away in 1994). She continues to work as a caregiver providing compassionate care to the elderly. Like her mother, helping others brings joy to her heart.

Beverly loves spending time with her daughter, sister, grandchildren, niece, and nephew. They are the light of her life!

Mrs. Zorata Talbert Basye

(Photo by Cheryl Basye)

*"Cheryl," she said. "You will not make
it on your looks. Looks fade."*

— Cheryl Basye

HONORING

Mrs. Zorata Talbert Basye

Written by Cheryl Basye / Daughter

Born in Oxford, MS in 1915, my mother was a fierce advocate for children and instilled in my brother, Raymond and me, a Christian spirit, an intense sense of our heritage, and an ability to see the world through the lens of truth and morality. She taught me to stand up for myself, have a healthy sense of humor, and not depend on physical characteristics to propel me forward. I was encouraged to develop my mind and personality so that I could contribute positively to everyone who came into my life. Her impact on my development gave me strength, tenacity, and a desire for continued personal development and for contributing to society.

Growing up in Oxford was difficult in the early 1900s, especially for fair-skinned women with light eyes and "good" hair. Mom was often mistaken for being White and her mother, whose skin was a chocolate hue, was often thought to be her nanny. Because of this dynamic, my mom sometimes found herself in a position of hearing disparaging things about the Black people in the community. As a result, she developed a powerful sense of Black pride in herself and her family at an early age.

After high school, Mom decided that she wanted to help children, so she chose to pursue a degree in education at Stowe Teachers College in St. Louis, MO. Shortly after she graduated, her cousin introduced her to a handsome and worldly young soldier, Raymond A. Basye. When her mother remarried a Baptist minister, Reverend S.L. Love, the family was plunged into a life centered around the church with strict rules about lifestyle. This had a great impact on young Zorata's life and courtship with my father. Their dates were closely monitored by my grandmother, who often sat in the living room clad in her nightgown and rollers to chaperone them. Her presence also ensured that the dates concluded at a reasonable time. My dad finally met all the tests, and they were married in 1944 and settled in St. Louis. On their brief honeymoon during one of his furloughs to New Orleans, my dad convinced Mommy to participate in the local "prettiest wife" beauty pageant. He was proud, but not at all surprised when his bride, Zorata, won the pageant.

My mom was vigilant about my brother and my academic and spiritual upbringing. She instilled in us that being part of God's community would help us to become better members of the community at large. She was superintendent of the Sunday School at Lane Tabernacle CME Church and encouraged us to be part of the youth programs and choir.

Mom eventually decided that she wanted to focus on working with children who had difficulty reading, so for three summers she went to Connecticut for graduate school and received her master's degree in Reading Education. After returning to the St. Louis public school system, she devoted herself not only to her students but also to her own children to ensure that their reading comprehension and verbal communication skills met or exceeded the standard. When she acquired tests to evaluate her students' reading proficiency, my brother and I were always the first test subjects. We never liked being guinea pigs for these tests, but all our teachers were impressed with how well we spoke and read, which we knew made my mom proud. I admired all that my mom was doing in church, her school, and the community.

Mom taught us to have pride in ourselves as beautiful Black children. One day, however, I took it too far by preening in the mirror. She stopped me short. "Cheryl," she said. "You will not make it on your looks. Looks fade. Learn to play the piano, and people will gather around you. Learn to know and understand current events. Show that you can engage in interesting conversations. These skills will attract others and bring good people into your life." I never forgotten these words. They have guided my relationships, although I'm afraid I may have disappointed her by never mastering piano playing.

When Mom found out that she had breast cancer, I saw her strength elevate to another level. She never complained. Her initial treatment was a radical mastectomy. I remember that she had to alter her strapless evening dresses by adding chiffon to cover the left side so that she could still wear them. She still looked very beautiful as she continued to go to events with my dad. Unfortunately, the mastectomy was not the cure we wanted, so my dad found a hospital in Denver, CO that was one of the early facilities to offer chemotherapy. While in Denver, Mom kept me updated on her treatments and amused me with her often comic commentary on the other patients but, she never once showed any weakness about her condition. Right before Thanksgiving, she wrote to let me know that the doctors were letting her come home for the holiday. She had one request from me . . . to get her a wig. The treatments had caused her to lose her hair.

When she arrived home, she was sitting in a wheelchair with the cutest hat on. She looked smaller to me, but her smile and energy were the same. One afternoon she asked me to come into the den where she was sitting in a recliner. She leaned back and said, "I want you to look at me as I close my eyes so that you can be strong when I die. When I go, you will need to be the strong one for your dad and brother." After what seemed like an eternity, she opened her eyes with a gentle smile on her face. She was preparing me for what was to come. That smile still gives me comfort and reminds me that she still loves me but is in heaven and happy. On December 5, 1965, my mother left us to be with God, and I hope she knows that, like her and because of her, I am still the strong one.

I continue to be active in the church and the community and, as she predicted, by developing myself I have attracted a cadre of interesting, wonderful, and accomplished friends and colleagues who enrich my life.

I love you, Mommy!

Cheryl Basye
Dallas, TX

Cheryl Basye
(Photo courtesy of Cheryl Basye)

Cheryl Renee Basye has had an expansive career as an educator, business executive, and entrepreneur and is a lifelong community service volunteer.

Cheryl developed and taught communication courses at Emerson College and the University of Rhode Island. She also developed the minority recruitment program for Radcliffe College.

As a business executive with Southland Corporation, Cheryl expanded the company's executive recruitment initiative to increase its pipeline of minority and women executives. She established its minority and women's business development program thereby opening opportunities for supplier relationships and mentorships for the corporate office and for its national chain of 7-Eleven stores.

Cheryl and her brother, Raymond Basye, won the city-wide non-food concessions contract for the Dallas Convention Center, Reunion Arena, and American Airlines Center to provide novelty merchandise management and sales for events at the venues and telecommunication services for conventions at the convention center. They also won the national contract to manage the Division I championships for the NCAA including such events as the Final Four and College World Series. She and Raymond later formed ZoCom Technologies, which provided telecommunications consulting, planning, and installations for Dallas-Fort Worth Airport and Love Field.

Cheryl has been an active community volunteer and has served on the boards of Dallas Big Brothers Big Sisters, the Black Caucus National Advisory Board, The Dallas Museum Minority Advisory Board, and The Dallas Summer Musicals. She has also served as a Presiding Judge for state and local elections in the Dallas metroplex.

Ms. Basye has a B.A. Degree in Education from Missouri University, and an MA in Business Education & Industrial Communications from Emerson College in Boston, MA. She has also completed the Minority Business Executive Program at The Tuck Business School, Dartmouth College. She received a Life Coach Certification from Ultimate Coach University and is a certified Myers Briggs practitioner.

Cheryl resides in Dallas, TX.

"My mother's love has always been
a sustaining force for our family,
and one of my greatest joys is seeing
her integrity, her compassion, her
intelligence reflected in my daughters."

Michele Obama

Mrs. Georgia Saunders and her daughter, Ingrid Saunders Jones

(Photo courtesy of Ingrid Saunders Jones)

"Never give up on a person you love. We all have our longs and shorts."

— Ingrid Saunders Jones

HONORING

Mrs. Georgia Lyles Saunders

Written by Ingrid Saunders Jones / Daughter

My mother, Georgia Lyles Saunders, died in 2014 at the age of ninety-nine. My life stopped for a while. I had to reset myself in the world and figure out how to move forward. It went something like this: right foot . . . left foot . . . breathe and repeat!

As I reflect upon that time, I realize that my mother taught me how to reset and move forward. You see, both of my brothers, with whom I grew up until my late 20s, died a year and a half apart. How does a mother survive that?! Her faith in God and love of me, my father, her twin grandsons, Derek and Erik, our extended family, and our love for her is what brought her through. My young nephews (her grandsons) helped her to restore focus and purpose to her role as a mother and grandmother. Reset accomplished! Her strength, devotion, and protection of me during that time are beyond description. There are no words to describe my mother's love accurately. It just WAS! It was ever-present, and it surrounded me. Her heart was tethered to my heart and soul.

My mother was born in Augusta, GA in 1915. Her mother, Blanche Sibert Lyles, was the mother of three girls and one boy. Mother was the oldest. They were reared in Tryon, NC in the beautiful Blue Ridge Mountains. Tryon is the place I visited in the summer. It was our "going down south" destination from Detroit, where I was born and reared.

Quality education was an absolute necessity for the Lyles children. Georgia and her siblings attended an elementary school started by her father at Tryon's Good Shepard Episcopal Church, the Lyles' family home church. She graduated from Knoxville College in 1936 with a degree in education. It was at Knoxville College that she met my father, Homer Saunders, whom she married in 1936. After marrying, they moved to Ann Arbor, MI where my father pursued and earned a master's degree from the University of Michigan.

My mother's professional career included teaching in North Carolina before her marriage, working as a social worker supervisor in the Detroit Welfare Department, serving as a counselor with the Comprehensive Employment and Training ACT program, and as a counselor with the city workforce training program. She has been described by those who worked with and for her as the "quintessential social worker." While working full-time, she obtained her master's degree in social work from Wayne State University.

*Ingrid Saunders Jones (middle) and her parents,
Georgia and Homer Saunders
(Photo courtesy of Ingrid Saunders Jones)*

Mother was a cultural aficionado. She enjoyed ballet, the theater, the symphony, and opera, and was a ravenous reader of books. She was also a member of Alpha Kappa Alpha Sorority, Inc. and the Knoxville College Alumni Club of Detroit.

Growing up, I went to ballet classes and performances and to Detroit's famous Fisher's Theater to see Harry Belafonte and Miriam Makeba perform. Our family went to see Diane Caroll, and Richard Kiley in the musical play, *No Strings*, and then we bought the LP album and played the soundtrack for weeks. We listened to a lot of music, from Duke Ellington and Sarah Vaughn to our favorite classical composers, Chopin, and Debussy. We saw the performances of *HAIR, Jesus Christ Super Star, Your Arms are Too Short to Box With God*, and *The Wiz*. Like my mother, I too, am an aficionado of the arts. So much so, that I have received an honorary degree from the Atlanta College of Arts (now Savannah College of Art and Design). This early exposure was a very important part of my educational experience. I didn't realize until much later that many young people did not have the same advantages. I am grateful to my parents for the sacrifices they made to afford me these opportunities. The arts continue to enrich my life immeasurably.

I followed in my mother's footsteps as an educator and youth advocate through my many affiliations, having a strong faith foundation, a love for the arts, and attaining a master's degree. We parted ways, however, when it came to sororities. She joined Alpha Kappa Alpha Sorority, Inc. and I joined Delta Sigma Theta Sorority, Inc. When she learned that I wanted to pledge Delta Sigma Theta Sorority, Inc. she did not object but encouraged me to follow my path and make my own choice. "Sorority is a function of place and time," she said.

One of the joys I will always treasure seeing my mother with her sisters, women who were very different in some ways but almost identical in intellect, manner, and style.

Indeed, they all reflected my grandmother's grit and determination to learn and succeed. I follow in their footsteps in this regard also.

As I put the pieces together, all of this goes back to my great-grandmother, who lived until I was fifteen. She was a warrior woman! I was told that when Plessy vs. Ferguson became the law of the land in 1896, my great-grandmother was furious. Her response to that indignity of "separate but equal" was to send her child, my grandmother, Blanche Lyles, to Paine College ten years later from which she graduated in 1910. I have her diploma and my mother's hanging in my home library. They continue to inspire me to move forward.

As is often said, success is the best response to injustice. From 1910 when my grandmother graduated, everyone in our ever-growing family, except two, have earned college degrees and most have graduate degrees also. My great-grandmother set our family on a trajectory from which we have all benefitted. Knowing that I come from a long line of strong, educated, focused, working women who prepared themselves and their families for the future makes me confident, focused, and determined to do my best and contribute to the betterment of society.

My mother taught me to be honest, kind, strong, and determined. Most of all, she modeled and insisted that I be a "lady" at all times. The operative phrase was "Let's not be common. We are not common in our speech, in our dress, or our behavior." An extension of that sentiment was expressed by my father early in my professional working life. He said to me: "Ingrid, you are going to realize that most of the people you'll work with are mediocre, your goal is not to be one of them. Be smart, be different, and don't follow the pack!" That's how our parents coached us, and it still makes me smile.

My mother worked, cooked dinner most nights, and made sure I was where I was supposed to be <u>on time</u>. Time was a big thing in our family. It was considered a sign of respect for people and events to be on time. It is still something that I adhere to and value.

My mother's words of wisdom:

- "You should always read and have a library of books that are special to you."

- "Never give up on a person you love. We all have our 'longs and shorts.'"

- "Your faith and church are the foundations of your personal strengths."

- "Always live below your means and keep some cash in your house."

My mother "knew" me in every aspect and phase of my life and did not hesitate to pull me up short when I seemed to be off course. She encouraged me to not be afraid to take risks and not be afraid of the future. She was my guide in this world. She guided me through successes but more importantly, she guided me through disappointments and losses. She did not judge mistakes harshly and she did not minimize emotional pain.

I hope I have conveyed how my mother made me feel. How her love cloaked me and poured strength and wisdom into me. She helped me to "spot" myself in this world. She set the tone for my life with her love, her voice, and the way she set a vision for my life.

Ingrid Saunders Jones
Atlanta, GA

Ingrid Saunders Jones
(Photo courtesy of Ingrid Saunders Jones)

Ingrid Saunders Jones is a respected global corporate leader, a champion of educational opportunity, and an advocate for empowered and healthy communities. In 2013, after over thirty years of leadership, Ms. Jones retired from The Coca-Cola Company as Senior Vice President of Global Community Connections and Chair of The Coca-Cola Foundation. During her years at the Company, Ms. Jones held roles of increasing responsibility and led a variety of important local, national, and global community initiatives.

Earlier in her career, Ms. Jones worked with the Honorable Maynard H. Jackson, the Mayor of the City of Atlanta; served as a legislative analyst for the president of the Atlanta City Council; served as Executive Director of the Detroit Wayne County Childcare Coordinating Council; and taught in the public schools of Detroit and Atlanta.

In 2012, Ms. Jones was elected as Chair of the National Council of Negro Women. She is credited with increasing membership and bringing fiscal solvency to the organization, during her six years of service as Chair. It was a highlight of her career to lead this magnificent organization of women and follow in the footsteps of its historic leaders, Dr. Mary McLoed Bethune, and Dr. Dorothy Irene Height.

Currently, Ms. Jones serves on the boards of the YWCA of Greater Atlanta and Clark Atlanta University. She is also a member of the Rotary Club of Atlanta, Delta Sigma Theta Sorority, Inc., the Links, Inc., and the Society of International Business Fellows.

A native of Detroit, Ms. Jones earned a bachelor's degree in education from Michigan State University and a master's degree in education from Eastern Michigan University. Her *Alma Mater*, Michigan State University, honored her with an honorary Doctorate of Humanities. She has also received honorary degrees from Spelman College, Knoxville College, the Atlanta College of Art, Morehouse School of Medicine, and Morris Brown College.

Mrs. Ruth Sanders-Reese

(Photo courtesy of Denise Reese)

"One of the most remarkable qualities of my mother is her ability to find joy and beauty in the simplest of moments."

— Denise Reese

HONORING

Mrs. Ruth Hazel Sanders-Reese

Written by Denise Reese / Daughter

As I sit down to reflect on the woman who has shaped my life in countless ways, I am overwhelmed with a flood of memories, emotions, and profound gratitude for Ruth Hazel Sanders-Reese. My mother, my guiding light, unwavering supporter, and rock, epitomizes selflessness, strength, and love. I am eternally grateful for the opportunity to express my deepest appreciation and admiration for the remarkable woman who has been my biggest cheerleader through every twist and turn of life's journey.

Growing up, I was keenly aware of the sacrifices my mother made for our family. She set aside her own dreams and aspirations, putting the needs of her husband and children above all else. Her unconditional love and unwavering dedication were evident in every aspect of her being. She is more than a mother: she is the heartbeat of our family, the glue that continues to hold us together through life's storms.

Despite the challenges and hardships that inevitably come with parenthood, my mother approached her role with grace, resilience, and boundless love. She navigated the highs and lows of motherhood with unwavering strength, always putting her children's well-being above her own. From bandaging scraped knees to offering sage advice during the tumultuous teenage years, she has and continues to be there for me and my brothers, every step of the way.

Our relationship, like any other, has had its fair share of ups and downs. There were moments of frustration, disagreement, and misunderstanding. Yet, through it all, my mother remained a steadfast pillar of support and love. She has taught me the value of forgiveness, compassion, and the importance of cherishing family above all else.

As I reflect on our journey together, I am filled with gratitude for the countless lessons my mother has taught me. She instilled in me the importance of hard work, perseverance, never losing sight of my dreams, and never despising small beginnings. Despite facing her own trials and tribulations, she approached life with an unwavering sense of optimism and resilience, inspiring me to do the same.

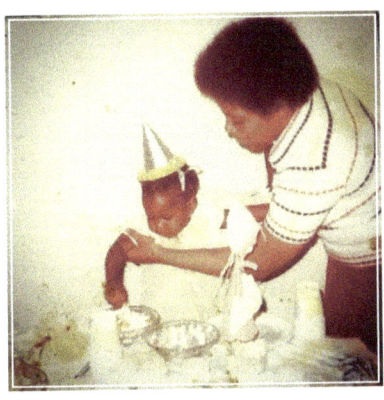

Denise Reese with her mother, Mrs. Ruth Reese
(Photo courtesy of Denise Reese)

One of the most remarkable qualities of my mother is her ability to find joy and beauty in the simplest of moments. Whether baking during the holidays, enduring countless international and domestic moves as a military family, making EVERY house a home, or sharing stories around the dinner table, she infused every moment with love, laughter, and warmth. Her presence has been a constant source of comfort and reassurance, a guiding light illuminating even the darkest of days.

As I navigate the complexities of adulthood, I find myself leaning on the wisdom and guidance imparted by my mother. Her words of encouragement and her gentle reminders to never lose sight of who I am, serve as a beacon of hope and inspiration. She continues to be my biggest cheerleader, celebrating my successes and offering unwavering support during life's inevitable setbacks.

In the tapestry of life, my mother's love is the thread that binds our family together, weaving a story of resilience, strength, and unwavering devotion. She has sacrificed so much to ensure that her children would have every opportunity to chase their dreams and pursue their passions. For that, and so much more, I am eternally grateful.

As I pen these words, I am filled with an overwhelming sense of love and appreciation for the remarkable woman who has shaped my life in immeasurable ways. To my mother: my rock, my confidante, and my greatest blessing, I offer my deepest gratitude and love. Thank you for being the embodiment of love, strength, and unwavering support. I am proud to be your daughter, forever and always.

Denise Reese
Atlanta, GA

Denise Reese

(Photo courtesy of Denise Reese)

Denise Reese is a Fractional Sales Executive and Founder and CEO of Grace The Collection™. She is a seasoned Business Development, Strategic Alliances, and Sales Executive in iconic branded, mid-market, and early-stage software and professional services companies.

Before launching her Fractional Executive career, Denise was Managing Director and South Market Unit Lead in the Accenture AWS Business Group (AABG.) AABG is a unique partnership that delivers transformation at scale with the best of AWS (Amazon Web Services,) and Accenture's unparalleled breadth and depth of talent, resources, and experience.

Denise has spent more than twenty-five years in Sales, Business Development, and Strategic Alliances roles for several IT Services and Software organizations and has held positions in both The United States and Europe. Her experience spans multiple disciplines including Identity and Access Management, IT Security, IT Outsourcing, Digital Transformation, and Cloud Computing.

Denise has built a brand rooted in developing trusted advisor relationships with her clients. This, coupled with a keen ability to build repeatable and sustainable revenue-generating opportunities, has allowed Denise to achieve significant milestones for the firms she's worked with. During her tenure with Wipro Technologies, a leading IT Services, Consulting, and Business Process Outsourcing Organization headquartered in Bangalore, India, she secured Wipro's first and largest Hospitality Client in the US and was a multi-million-dollar contributor to the RCTG (Retail, CPG, Transportation, and Government) Business Unit. While at Amazon Web Services, Denise was an award-winning Senior Customer Practice Manager in AWS Professional Services and built a multi-million-dollar portfolio in the Southeast market.

In 2020, Denise decided to leverage her decades-long experience leading and growing businesses globally for others, to start her own company, Grace The Collection™, a luxury home fragrance line. Grace The Collection was founded out of Denise's love for creating everyday-accessible luxury, and, to create a curated community to remind us to extend grace to ourselves and each other! Denise holds an MBA in Strategic Management from The Henley Business School in The United Kingdom, and her dissertation research focused on the importance of businesses adopting a sound IT Security and Risk policy. During her MBA Program, she completed her International Business Experience in Hong Kong. This allowed her the opportunity to analyze and provide strategic direction to Asia-Pacific companies in multiple industries including manufacturing, retail, and the public sector.

Denise is passionate about serving in the community and embodies the qualities of a true Servant Leader. She currently serves on the Board of Directors for Girl Scouts of Greater Atlanta. Denise is also past President of the Women in Technology (WIT) Foundation Board, the philanthropic arm of WIT, Inc. She has also served as Board Chair for Cool Girls, Inc. and was a founding Board Member and Director of Development for the Greater Atlanta Professional Chapter of Women MBA's International, formerly known as the National Association of Women MBA's. Denise was named a TAG Hub Magazine GA Game Changer in STEM Education and is a graduate of Leadership Atlanta, Class of 2017.

Shirley McEwen (standing) and her mother, Mrs. Audrey McEwen

(Photo courtesy of Shirley McEwen)

"When I had a problem or concern, Mama was the one person I could always turn to."

— Shirley McEwen

HONORING

Mrs. Audrey Pearl Cook McEwen

Written by Shirley McEwen / Daughter

I was the youngest of two daughters. My mother, Audrey Pearl Cook McEwen, was my inspiration in life and my role model. I learned to cook and clean and how be a good mother by observing her devotion to my siblings and me. Mama not only cooked the our meals, but she brought it to the table so that we could eat as a family.

My mother had a sense of trust that could not be broken. When I had a problem or concern, Mama was the one person I could always turn to. I was shy compared to my older sister and my mother sometimes expressed the hope that someday, I would become more assertive and do what I felt was best rather than relying on the actions of others. My mother's wish for me has come true. Even though other members of my family made it clear they would always be there for me, I am now able to work through my own issues. I am now an independent and confident woman because of my mother's support and encouragement.

What stands out to me about my mother is her outlook on life, her generosity, her sense of humor, civic duty, compassion, and wisdom. I did not learn in school as quickly as my siblings, however, my mother never made me feel inferior. She always encouraged me to just do the very best I could. I was tall and self-conscious about my height growing up. Mama let me know that I was fine and should not worry because I would someday appreciate my height and size. I also recall worrying about my birthday because it was in November and was the last in the family for the year. My mother's birthday was in March so she told me that she could switch with me so I would have two birthdays a year. I did not have a lot of material things, but I had unconditional love from my mother. I always stuck by her side even through adulthood.

My mother put her life on hold to take care of her children. Growing up I watched her walk back and forth to jobs so that she could provide for the five of us. She never complained, she just did what she knew had to be done. Anyone who knows me will tell you that I am a hard worker also.

I grew up with a mother who respected herself and her children. She cherished her time with us. She also made a point to attend church and see to it that all her children attended as well. Mama taught us to take care of each other and to keep the family close.

We loved and respected our mother because of the way she carried herself. There was no such thing as showing disrespect in our household.

Mrs. Audrey McEwen and her daughter, Shirley McEwen
(Photo courtesy of Shirley McEwen)

Taking care of my grandmother, Eudora Pearl Cook, was also important to my mother. My grandmother did not want to be placed in a home so Mama brought her into our home so that she could take care of her. As I watched Mama take care of her mother, I knew I would never let my mother need anything. As she got older and unable to care for herself, I took care of her in the same way that she took care of my grandmother. Each time Mama was admitted to the hospital, I stayed with her. There was never a time when she was alone. I will not take all the credit, but I did what I could. I have tried to put into practice what I learned from my mother by respecting myself and providing my children and grandchildren with the same unconditional love, respect, and support that I received from my mother.

My mother was unique and irreplaceable. Our bond was unconditional and cannot be placed into words. As I look over my life, I can see my mother in me in so many ways.

Shirley McEwen
Pascagoula, MS

Shirley McEwen
(Photo courtesy of Shirley McEwen)

Shirley McEwen was born and raised in Pascagoula, MS. After high school, she briefly attended Mississippi Gulf Coast Community College and the University of Southern Mississippi. She graduated from Ms. Jones Cosmetology School and immediately began working as a stylist in a local salon. Even though she was the only African American in the salon, her skillful styling garnered her a large, diverse clientele. She soon moved out of that shop and opened a salon of her own, Skillet's Barber and Beauty Shop.

After starting a family, Shirley decided to accept a full-time job as a financial service representative at National American Corporation where she worked for twelve years. She worked in the salon only on weekends. In 1995 Shirley began working at Singing River Health System as a collector and, within a few years, she was promoted to the position of supervisor. A few years after starting there, she was appointed as a financial counselor in the hospital's Cancer Center where she remains after twenty-nine years.

Shirley is a very active member of her community and church, St. Mark United Methodist Church. St. Mark was built by her great-grandfather, and he served as a Trustee. Four generations of her family have worshiped and served at St. Mark and Shirley currently serves as the Worship Committee Chairperson. Over the years, she has also served as Youth Coordinator, Youth Coordinator for Community Outreach, Administrative Board Chairperson, and Treasurer. Shirley has taken several youth groups to nursing homes to provide the residents with gift bags for Christmas. She looks forward to the Annual Family and Friends Day when friends and family from around the city and country return to worship and fellowship with their home church community. As church Treasurer, it is also gratifying for her to record their generous contributions.

Shirley participates in Bra's Across the River for cancer patients each year, Relay for Life, the Heart Walk, the Love Big 5K, Sunset on Cancer Run, and the March of Dimes' annual event. She is the proud and devoted mother of three children: Erica, Eric, Jr., and Chantel as well as three grandchildren. They are the light of her life and keep her very busy as she shares in their many activities.

Gail Broadwater, Mrs. Mary Broadwater, and Joyce Broadwater

(Photo courtesy of Joyce Broadwater)

"Mary Broadwater would give you her last dollar if you needed it or the blouse off her back, as she encourages you not to give up. I am not like her in that way."

— Joyce Broadwater

HONORING

Mrs. Mary Julia Broadwater

Written by Joyce Broadwater / Daughter

I am my mother's daughter. I have been told this frequently! When I think about my mother, I cannot help but think of her as a strong Black woman. She instilled self-confidence in me at a very early age as she repeatedly assured me, "You can do it, Joyce." That encouragement has served me well over the years. Even today as an adult, when I am confronted with a daunting task, I can still "hear" my mom saying, "You can do it!" It doesn't matter what "it" is, I am empowered by her faith in me. Because of her, I know that whatever I am going through, I will emerge okay.

Lately, more and more people tell me that I look like my mother. I am also told that I act like her! I'm not so sure about that because, in my opinion, my mother's shoes are hard to fill. She exemplifies motherhood to me. Mary Broadwater would give you her last dollar if you needed it or the blouse off her back, as she encourages you not to give up. I am not like her in that way. Although I am generous, I will not be giving you my last dollar.

I am the oldest of three children including a younger sister and brother. I know that some mothers appear to have a favorite child, however, I sincerely believe that my mom loves all three of us deeply and equally. So much so, that at times, I believe my mother can even feel our physical pain.

One of my most vivid memories is when I got ready to leave home for college. We had a see-through burglar door at the back of the house. As my dad and I got into the car to leave for my flight to Washington, D.C., Mom literally could not leave the house. She was frozen behind the burglar door with tears streaming down her face. This sight left me conflicted and teary. I didn't want to leave her standing there. I was excited, however, to start my college journey at Howard University and my dad, who knew that the delay would not help, urged me to hurry and get in the car. He knew that she would eventually adjust to this new reality and would be alright.

When I was in elementary school, I recall that my mom worked hard to raise funds for my sister to become "Miss Pryor Street," a neighborhood fundraising endeavor. She cooked and sold fried fish and chitlin plates, and made red candied apples to sell. Her mission was accomplished! She raised the most money and my sister, Gail, was crowned with the "coveted" title. Mom was always our biggest champion and supportive of everything we did.

My mother once told me that courage has been an essential element of her life. She shared that in the early '70s a man knocked on the door and when she answered it, he pointed a gun at her. She swiftly tried to close the door but was unsuccessful. Fortunately (or unfortunately!), my little sister who was home sick that day, ran into the living room when she heard the commotion. This frightened the man, and he retreated and ran away. If this had been me, at this point, I would have called the police. Not my mom. She took my sister across the street to a retired neighbor's house, and she and our neighbor's husband, Mr. Campbell, left with his gun to go look for the guy! This is what I call fortitude! Some would call it crazy, but my mother's protective instincts are just that strong. This scenario probably would not work out so well today. I thank God for keeping her and my sister alive that day. I do not want to imagine what my life would have been like without her.

Although my mother is the only daughter of four children, she comes from a long line of strong, Black, hardworking, industrious, and humorous women. She has always longed to have sisters. To some degree, she found them at church in the Order of the Eastern Star and our extended family and friends.

Mom has never met a stranger. It never ceases to amaze me how many people know her. She is affectionately known as "Ms. Mary." While walking down the street in New York a few years ago, we heard someone yell "Hey Ms. Mary." Over the years, she has touched many people through her kind and generous spirit. Many of them consider her to be their mom also.

Both of my parents started businesses. My mom owned a hair salon on the infamous Peachtree Street in Atlanta, GA for eighteen years. There, she nurtured, trained, and blessed many people who worked in her shop. Many went on to open shops of their own. Like my mother, I am supportive and encouraging to others. I work very hard in my sorority, Alpha Kappa Alpha, Inc., and in other organizations to promote sisterhood and empower other Black women by sharing my knowledge, resources, and contacts with them. My father was a road construction contractor and built roads and parking lots for many years. I worked for him for a year after I finished college. I learned from both my parents, and, because of their examples, I am a serial entrepreneur. I have owned several businesses, but real estate has remained constant. As a realtor, it has been my goal to help as many Black people as possible to own homes.

My mom has a spirit of humility that is second to none. My sister and I used to get upset when she sometimes shared her time with other people in need. Our home has sheltered numerous cousins and has been a haven for many others over the years.

We used to fondly call it "Hotel California." Mom has helped pay school tuition, buy baby formula, cook dinners, and clothe kids to help friends, neighbors, and family. She loves and is passionately protective of all children. One of my fondest memories was seeing her reaction when she saw her two granddaughters for the first time. She LOVES her grandkids!

My mom was a caretaker for her mom and my father in their final days. She is a praying woman who is like the Energizer Bunny®-she just keeps on going. This woman has helped me to be a courageous, empathic, and caring mother. I have tried to teach these same virtues to my only child. I will soon see if I have been successful, as I am about to experience my next chapter in life as a grandmother in early 2024.

Joyce Broadwater
Conyers, GA

Joyce Broadwater
(Photo courtesy of Joyce Broadwater)

Joyce Broadwater has been working in financial services for over twenty-five years with an emphasis on mortgages and real estate.

Joyce holds a master's in public administration from Troy University and a bachelor's in finance from Howard University. She is also a graduate of the United Way VIP Program.

She enjoys helping people reach their goals of becoming homeowners. Her passion for helping others understand credit is sparked whenever she meets a person who is struggling with understanding how to navigate the credit maze.

Joyce has worked as a Regional Manager of Provident Bank, as an Urban Mortgage Consultant for Wachovia Mortgage, and as Executive Director of the South Dekalb Small Business Incubator. She owned Hair With Flair Salon for five years. Immediately out of college, she worked for two years as Business Manager for Broadwater Construction owned by her father. She is currently the owner and broker of Broadwater Home Group, LLC.

Joyce is a life coach who enjoys conducting training programs, workshops, and seminars in strategic planning, team building, people development, credit, and non-profit operations. As an entrepreneur, she has built businesses from the bottom up. Joyce has been recognized as a "Trailblazer" by her peers in her field of real estate.

Ms. Broadwater is a licensed Georgia real estate agent, a Certified Emerging Markets Specialist, and a Certified Fanny Mae and FHA Specialist. She has also had training in mortgage fraud detection, a member of the Empire Board of Realtists, Dekalb Association Board of Realtors, and a dedicated member of Alpha Kappa Alpha Sorority, Inc.

"Black moms create magic, so
that makes me magical."

Stephanie Lahart

Mrs. Cheryl Lewis Mines

(Photo courtesy of Cheryl Mines)

*"My mother, Cheryl Mines, taught me how
to be a woman and daughter of God."*

— Andrea Christine Mines

HONORING

Mrs. Cheryl Lewis Mines

Written by Andrea Christine Mines / Daughter

My mother, Chery Mines, taught me how to be a woman and daughter of God. She always leads by example in the way she carries herself, speaks to others, and cares for her family. As a young person today, self-respect and humility are counter-cultural traits that can be easily lost amid social media and fast fashion.

Elitism was never acceptable to my mother. She believes that everyone should do their best and taught me that "best" will look different for each person. She also taught me that the people we surround ourselves with should treat us in a way that acknowledges and appreciates our value. For that reason, we should not have personal relationships with people who do not respect us.

My mother always reinforced these lessons by her example. She took us with her to volunteer activities and encouraged us to engage with our community. She was constantly researching and learning new things. Most of all, she has been blessed with loyal friends through every season of her life. She has a wonderful support system and sets a great example for how we can construct our lives as adults.

The values that my mom taught me are not always the most popular ones in society. She prepared me to encounter sideway glances and overt attempts to stop my success without doubting myself or folding to criticism. I learned to keep my head up and stay on my path because I can have complete faith in God's plan for my life. I may need to set boundaries or have difficult conversations, but everything can and should be done with kindness, keeping in mind that every human being deserves respect. Mommy cultivated my ability to judge character and demanded that I stop to think critically before making any decision. I learned not to fear something just because it's challenging because challenges help us to grow and learn. As I have grown into my voice and womanhood, I have peace and self-confidence when challenged because I know that my work is only for the Lord. I work in the STEM field as a chemist, and these lessons come to my mind with each encounter.

Andrea Mines and her mother, Cheryl Mines

Chemistry is a challenging discipline, and the learning environment does not facilitate the success of Black women. This challenge motivates me and makes me even more determined to pursue Chemistry as a career. Many people in the scientific space find my presence intimidating, but when the days get hard, I can always call my mom who fills me back up with love and restores my confidence and determination. As an accounting manager, she is also in a STEM occupation, so she understands my challenges and provides informed and sage advice.

I am so grateful for my mother's high expectations of her three daughters to be excellent, modest, and kind, woven between the soft touches and comforts that only a mother can provide. My mom is my touchstone when times are hard and I need to be reminded of my fortitude and value, and she always pushes me to be my very best. I feel incredibly blessed that God gifted my mother to me. Because of my mother, I am a strong, kind, intellectual woman of faith, and I am excited to one day pass these values on to the next generation. Words cannot truly express who my mother is to me, but her love could not have more perfectly shaped me into the person I am today.

Andrea Christine Mines
Pittsburgh, PA

Andrea Mines
(Photo courtesy of Cheryl Mines)

Andrea Christine Mines is a native of the Atlanta area. She received a B.A. in Chemistry from Boston University (BU) in 2021. While at BU, Andrea's research, *Nanobodies for Medical Imaging: About Ready for Prime Time?* was published in Biomedical, in April of 2021. She is currently pursuing a Ph.D. in Chemistry at the University of Pittsburgh while also conducting cutting-edge research in High-Performance Liquid Chromatography. Her scientific skills include Mass Spectrometry, Nuclear Magnetic Resonance, UV/Vis Spectrometry, and physical, organic, and general chemistry. Andrea plays the saxophone and clarinet. She enjoys reading, music, spending time with her family (especially her one-year-old nephew, Shaiyah), and playing with her cat.

Mrs. Thelma Smith Lewis

(Photo courtesy of Marlena Lewis-Mohr)

*"There's no emotion I can't show to her and
no subject I can't talk with her about."*

— Marlena Lewis-Mohr

HONORING

Mrs. Thelma Smith Lewis

Written by Marlena Lewis-Mohr / Daughter

The relationship between my mom, Thelma Smith Lewis, and me is one that I truly never expected. First, we couldn't be more different. She's cool, calm, and collected. She's slow to anger and gracious enough to give you a fair warning (a.k.a. "the look") when her boundaries are about to be crossed. My mom is confident with an indomitable spirit second only to her mother, my grandma, Anna. I am 100% none of this.

I'm the anxious one worrying about one thing or another. I've got the loud, outgoing spirit of my dad's side of the family but I'm incredibly shy speaking in public, especially if all eyes are on me. Except for a "lil attitude," our laughs, and a decent sense of style that we have in common, even my mom jokes that I'm not hers.

Marlena Lewis-Mohr and her mother, Mrs.Thelma Lewis
(Photo courtesy of Marlena Lewis-Mohr)

Despite all my perceived shortcomings in not being just like her, I couldn't have asked for a better, more positive role model than my mama. I've stumbled and failed countless times, but she has never held my disappointments over my head or tried to shame me. Instead, she showed her compassion and offered her advice whenever I asked for or needed it. We've both had our fair share of immense heartaches and overwhelming loss. But somehow, despite her own struggles and pain, she has managed to remain the immovable rock her children and family could cling to most when they felt they were drowning in despair.

Commitment, loving unconditionally, and loving fiercely; are the things she taught me through her actions and her words. There's no emotion I can't show to her and no subject I can't talk with her about. For the nearly forty years of my life, my mom has been my safe space.

Our love and mutual respect matured through a long, slow process. Through all the laughter, tears, and even anger, the relationship Mama and I have built has always thrived on open and honest communication without judgment. As a mother myself, I can now see how powerful and incredibly important it is to have a mother's unwavering and ever-constant support. Showing love by having her words and actions match, is still the most invaluable lesson she ever taught me. It is a gift and a blessing.

Marlena Lewis-Mohr
Munich, Germany

Marlena Lewis-Mohr
(Photo courtesy of Marlena Lewis-Mohr)

Marlena Lewis-Mohr is a graduate of Florida State University in music education and German studies. She has been living in Munich, Germany for more than eight years and currently works at International House for Kids as a kindergarten English teacher and as a freelance English as a Second Language (ESL) teacher for adults at Berlitz Language School Germany in Munich.

Malena plays piano and saxophone. She and her husband hope that their love of travel and music will rub off on their three-year-old daughter, Mayla. Marlena also hopes that Mayla will read these stories and find inspiration in, and appreciation for, the wonderfully unique women in this anthology, her family, and the world.

*Jenae Holloway and her
mother, Dr. Jeanette Sabir-Holloway*

*"Though I didn't express it at the time, that night
became etched in my memory – a testament to my
mom's intuitive understanding of my needs."*

— Jenae Holloway

HONORING

Dr. Jeanette Sabir-Holloway

Written by Jenae Holloway / Daughter

Dr. Jeanette Sabir-Holloway

(Photo courtesy of Jenae Holloway)

When I discovered that I was pregnant, I immersed myself in the world of mommy apps only to be inundated by the whirlwind of decisions – from choosing diapers and strollers to navigating the intricacies of night nannies and gentle parenting. The abundance of advice from mommy bloggers and mommy friends, each with their own adamant views on how to survive the newborn phase, left me feeling utterly overwhelmed. Just as I was trying to adjust to the idea of pregnancy, I found myself grappling with choices that seemed to shape not only my future but also my identity as a mother-to-be.

During my identity crisis, I stumbled upon a concept, born on TikTok, that defines various archetypes of moms in my generation. There were the "Crunchy" moms, advocates of cloth diapers, homemade organic baby food, and the immune-boosting powers of breastmilk over vaccines. Conversely, the "Silky" moms are unafraid of epidurals and readily embrace modern conveniences like Tylenol and a McDonald's Happy Meal. Between these extremes are the "Scrunchie" moms, who use organic formula and give their children vaccinations, albeit on a delayed schedule. Despite being in my mid-thirties, the sheer weight of motherhood's demands caught me off guard, making me wonder about my own mother's parenting identity and how she juggled the pressure of managing her dental practice, raising two children, and supporting her husband at the same time.

It dawned on me that my mother couldn't be neatly categorized; she embodies aspects of each archetype while also *transcending* them altogether. She was a "Crunchy" mom, faithfully frequenting organic stores and forcing us to put wheat germ into our yogurt every morning. At the same time, she embraced the mindset of a "Silky" mom, skillfully navigating the demands of a career in the 80s with the help of a nanny and a Gameboy. But that's not all, my mom is also the fun mom, the empathetic mom, the warm yet firm mom, the reliable mom, the stylish mom, the spontaneous mom, the chronically-late-for-pick-up-mom, and the cool but *"not one of your little friends"* mom. Rather than adhering to rigid parenting doctrines, my mom relied on intuition honed by her own upbringing, carving out her own path. Her maternal identity is fluid, adapting seamlessly to the unique needs of each person she has touched.

During my high school years, Friday night basketball games held immense social significance. Like any typical teenager, I was keenly focused on fitting in and expanding my circle of friends. It felt like destiny when the biggest game of the year fell on my birthday. As I rifled through my closet in search of the perfect outfit, I daydreamed about the potential to meet my next boyfriend, forge countless connections, and solidify my status as an "It Girl" in my city. However, my excitement quickly turned to disbelief as my mom informed me that we were attending an etiquette class at the Skyline Club that same Friday night. After unsuccessfully pleading with her for days to reconsider, I resigned myself to what felt like cruel and unusual punishment, particularly on my birthday. To my relief, when we arrived at the club, I realized that the etiquette class was merely a ruse. Two of my closest friends from middle school had been invited to join us for dinner, instantly transforming what I had anticipated to be a dull evening discussing manners over *crudités*, into a heartwarming reunion as we laughed and gossiped over fries and chicken fingers.

Later, my mom surprised us with tickets to the musical "Mamma Mia!" I had always loved musicals, albeit secretly, as it conflicted with my "cool girl" image in high school. I had become a little lost under the weight of high school's social pressures, prioritizing boys, and makeup over the earnest joy of singing and dancing to show tunes. However, that night, as we unabashedly belted out songs from the soundtrack on the ride home, I came to understand the profound impact of my mom's thoughtful gesture. It not only reignited my passion for theater, but it provided me a safe space to reconnect to my truest self. Though I didn't express it at the time, that night became etched in my memory, a testament to my mom's intuitive understanding of my needs. She was the kind of mom who didn't always give me what I wanted, but always gave me exactly what I needed.

My mom's transition into motherhood appeared effortless and natural, like she was always destined to be a mom. Growing up with seventeen siblings (blended family) had primed her for caregiving, but her nurturing instincts were always deeply ingrained and extended beyond familial ties. Her magnetic energy has drawn people from all walks of life into our home seeking support and guidance. Our kitchen has become a hub for hosting baby showers and family reunions and a sanctuary for heart-to-heart conversations over a glass of wine during some of life's most difficult moments. I've witnessed her unwavering attention as my friends confided in her, revealing vulnerabilities and secrets that they wouldn't even disclose to their own mothers, sharing struggles with co-parenting, anxieties about pursuing higher education, and grappling with relationship infidelity.

In her professional life, Mom not only champions diversity but also provides motherly support to her students, assuming roles of counselor, mentor, financial advisor, and even realtor when needed. While she may not have all the answers, she has the innate ability to provide a sense of security and reassurance that outweighs any predicament, affirming that everything will eventually fall into place. And despite her capacity to nurture countless individuals, she still has limitless energy to dedicate to her own children and grandchildren. She remains the beating heart at the center of our family unit.

As I continue to navigate motherhood, I hope to craft my own distinct approach also, drawing inspiration from the compassionate and graceful example set by my mom. I want my son to view me as a haven where he can be his most honest and authentic self, knowing that I will always offer empathy and understanding whenever he seeks guidance or consolation. I imagine our home as a welcoming gathering spot for our friends and family to share stories and laughter over margaritas and a game of Spades on Saturday nights. Like my mom, I hope my son appreciates that while I may not always grant his every wish, I will always instinctively provide what he truly needs. Most of all, I hope he sees my mother's reflection in me. I hope to carry on her legacy with grace and love.

Jenae Holloway
New York, New York

Jenae Holloway
(Photo courtesy of Jenae Holloway)

Jenae Holloway is a creative strategist, event producer, and writer who specializes in the intersection between storytelling, popular culture, and social impact. Before joining EBONY as Director of Special Events, Jenae was the Associate Director of Special Events at *Vogue,* where she produced the CFDA/Vogue Fashion Fund Gala, the Tony Awards red carpet, and the Costume Institute Benefit (Met Gala). In her earlier years at Conde Nast, Jenae was the Special Projects Editor at *Glamour* where she developed programming for the Glamour Women of the Year Awards, produced two global panel discussions with First Lady Michelle Obama, and wrote about education inequality, racial justice, and Black culture. Jenae lives in Brooklyn with her partner and her son, "Beau".

"Next to God, we are indebted to women, first for life itself, and then for making it worth living."

Dr. Mary McLeod Bethune

Mrs. Ernestine Siggers Berry

(Photo courtesy of The Honorable Constance Newman)

*"Mother made every day
an interesting day."*

— Constance ("Connie") Berry Newman, Esq.

HONORING

Mrs. Ernestine Siggers Berry

Written by Constance "Connie" Berry Newman, Esq. / Daughter

My mother (and father) prepared me to live a meaningful life, as did they. They made a difference on this earth in so many ways. My parents were an effective team, but I will only express my observations about my mother in this essay.

Ernestine Siggers Berry was born in Minneapolis, MN, where, throughout her childhood, she was the only African American in her schools. She finished elementary and high school in Minneapolis and went on to complete nursing and social work studies in Chicago where she met my father. They completed their family with two girls and one boy, all successful in their professions of choice.

Ernestine's deep interest in the life and history of African Americans led our family to move to Tuskegee, AL, where she led the Red Cross, and my surgeon father led the NAACP. I share that history because it explains why I am who I am, why I care about what I care about, and why I work to accomplish what I try very hard to accomplish.

Below is a set of words and phrases that best describe my mother, Ernestine.

- *Principled and Religious*: Life has not been overly complicated for me because our parents taught us basic rules about right and wrong and that lying, cheating, and stealing were all just plain wrong! We also knew that any move in the direction of "wrong" would end up with great punishments, primarily "the silent treatment," which was the most painful.

- *Smart and Wise*: Mother was always reading, studying, and questioning someone about everything. What was important was that she analyzed her "book learning" with practical applications. She often said that if it is wrong, it is generally hard to explain and even harder to do. That simple concept led me away from doing most wrong things.

- *Interesting, Fun, and Funny*: Mother made every day an interesting day. Every evening at dinner, she had a new bit of information for us to discuss. And we were often quizzed on information from previous meals. Four times a year, the entire decoration of the house was changed to reflect the season. Every holiday was celebrated with special meals of that holiday and the history of the holiday was included in the evening's discussion.

- **Giving, Sharing, and Loving**: Until the day she died, Mother gave to others. Thanksgiving, New Year's Day, Halloween, and every holiday or event, generally ended up with people at the table we had never met who had not received any other invitation to share the holiday. All were treated as if they were family. We were expected to give to others: money, food, time, and effort.

The Berry Family (left to right)
Joeann, Mrs. Ernestine and Dr. Joseph Berry
Constance and Joseph, Jr.
(Photo courtesy of Constance Newman)

Mrs. Earnestine Berry with daughters Constance (left) and Joeann
(Photo courtesy of Constance Newman)

After my father died in his 50s, I tried to find a partner for her. Mother always called me "Constance." So, after calling my name, she said to me: "Stop bringing these sad, broken-down men to meet me! I can never replace your father; the men you find are too needy. Granted, I am a nurse and social worker, but I am not looking for patients." That was the end of my match-making project.

When Mother moved to Washington from Tuskegee just before my surprise divorce, she and I got together once a week for a play, a museum visit, or dinner at a special restaurant, including time to make up stories about the people who passed by.

I think about Ernestine Siggers Berry almost every day because she was my mother, teacher, leader, and best friend. I miss her.

Constance "Connie" Berry Newman, Esq.
Washington, D.C.

The Honorable Constance Newman
(Photo courtesy of Constance Newman)

The Honorable Constance Berry Newman has had extensive experience in developing and managing policies and programs for the United States government, the Government of the District of Columbia, and organizations in the international arena. At present, she is advising the African Development Foundation on establishing programs in Somalia. Also, she is the Special Counsel to the Carmen Group on African Affairs. Seven of the Federal government positions she has held were Presidential appointments, five required Senate confirmations.

Her past positions in the federal government include Director of the Office of Personnel Management, Assistant Secretary of Consumer and Regulatory Affairs in the Department of Housing and Urban Development; Vice Chair of the Consumer Product Safety Commission; and Director of VISTA. Between 1992 and 2000, she served as the Under Secretary of the Smithsonian Institution. For the District of Columbia government, Newman served as Vice Chair of the Control Board that managed the city government from 1994 to 2001. In the international arena, Newman served as Assistant Secretary of State for African Affairs and Assistant Administrator for Africa at the United States Agency for International Affairs from 2001 to 2005. During that period, she was the Personal Representative of the President of the United States to the G8 on Africa. She has also worked as a project director for the World Bank and as a member of the Board of the International Republican Institute monitoring elections and democracy-building activities in Nigeria, Ukraine, Russia, Kenya, Afghanistan, Liberia, Bangladesh, and China. Newman is a graduate of Bates College in Government (A.B.) and the University of Minnesota Law School (B.S.L.). She was a member of the Adjunct Faculty at the Kennedy School, Harvard University, from 1979 to 1982. She is currently an Adjunct Professor in the Department of

Government at George Washington University where she teaches courses on leadership. Constance Newman is listed in *TheHistoryMakers.*

Mrs. Claretta Lewis

(Photo courtesy of Claretta Kerns)

"Ma had this great personality but when it was time for decorum and soberness, she had no problem behaving as the occasion required."

— Claretta Kerns, Ed.D.

HONORING

Mrs. Claretta Teresa Antone Lewis

Written by Claretta Kerns, Ed.D. / Daughter

I have always thought that I possess many of my mother's traits, her personality, and her "ways." Perhaps it's because I am named after her but, then again, it may be because of her influence during my formative years.

As far back as I can remember "Ma," as we affectionately called her, was always a fun-loving, jovial, high-spirited individual. When "Clara" arrived at family gatherings, everyone knew that she was "in the house." During the holiday season, we would really see that manifested as she entered the annual Antone (her family) gatherings joyfully proclaiming, "Christmas cheer!" And, oh yes, the party was on! I definitely inherited my love for family and its importance from my mother, and I am so grateful for that. Whenever there is the slightest opportunity to get with my siblings and family, I am in the midst, and when I arrive, everyone knows that the party has begun and "Lil' Clara is in the house." Ma was known as "Big Clara" by her mom, and I was called "Lil' Clara." I not only had her name but was called by a derivative of her nickname as well. This was and remains my identity. I carry both proudly!

Ma enjoyed herself in almost every situation. She never met a stranger. Our dad recalled that while riding downtown on the public bus, he would stand, and Ma would sit down next to someone. During the ride, she would engage in conversation with the person sitting next to her. After reaching their destination, Dad would ask Ma who the woman was that she had been talking to for thirty minutes, to which she would respond, "I don't know." That is how easily she bonded with people.

Growing up, I particularly enjoyed our visits with Ma's sisters. Listening to their banter, joking around, and storytelling was so entertaining, that is, until they had to share "grown folk talk" and the children were dismissed. Ma was quite a talker, and she could really tell a story, complete with details and embellishments. I love to do the same thing when my sisters and I gather. This is another way that my behavior emulates hers.

Ma was a God-fearing, deeply religious woman who loved her husband, her children, and her family. While enduring mental health issues, her faith remained strong and she consistently, tenaciously, and earnestly pleaded with us to make sure we accepted Jesus Christ as our personal savior. She also stressed the need for and the power of prayer.

Claretta Kerns and mother, Mrs. Claretta Lewis
(Photos courtesy of Claretta Kerns and Paulette Lewis)

To this day, I look back at her testimony as reassurance of God's faithfulness. He will answer ALL prayers, in His time and according to His will. I saw that manifested in her metamorphosis when the Lord brought her out of the darkness of clinical depression and returned our fun-loving Ma to the family.

Before her battle with clinical depression, Ma was such a fun-loving and entertaining person. I would categorize myself the same way and I believe that my siblings, nieces, and nephews would also. Now, please do not misunderstand. Ma had this great personality but when it was time for decorum and soberness, she had no problem behaving as the occasion required. She was hardworking, thrifty, not wasteful, and virtuous. I aspire to be and am perceived the same way by my family and friends.

Ma had great expectations and ambitions for her children. There was no such thing as failing. She was a proud woman and always held her head high, but not in a conceited or selfish way. She was very proud of her nine children also, and she had a way of making each of us know that we were special. She encouraged all of us to reach higher academically and aspire to rewarding careers. I remember a few anecdotes that reflect her encouragement, however, the one that stands out is about how she regularly asked all her children: "What do you want to be when you grow up?" Initially I proudly responded. "I want to be a housewife, just like you!" She quickly retort: "No, you don't! You want to be a businesswoman or a teacher. I want you to go to college."

I often reflect on the fact that I did indeed achieve both and that she would be proud. I am so happy that she was able to see me receive my undergraduate degree. I only regret that she was not alive to see me receive a doctorate in education or to see the innovative early college program that I launched several years ago. As a result of this program, first-generation students who may not have the strong parental advocate that we did, are provided experiences to boost their confidence and strengthen their college entrance qualifications.

The Proverbs 31 scripture is so apropos for Ma. "She is clothed with strength and dignity; she can laugh at the days to come. She speaks with wisdom, and faithful instruction is on her tongue. She watches over the affairs of her household and does not eat the bread of idleness. Her husband has full confidence in her and lacks nothing of value. She brings him good, not harm, all the days of her life. She opens her arms to the poor and extends her hands to the needy. When it snows, she has no fear for her household; for all of them are clothed in scarlet."

Claretta Kerns, Ed.D.
Duncan, SC

Dr. Claretta Kerns
(Photo courtesy of Dr. Claretta Kerns)

Dr. Claretta Kerns is the Dean of Spartanburg County Early College High School in Spartanburg, SC. She has academic, programmatic, managerial, and fiscal responsibilities for the 9th through 12th grade facility on a college campus. She leads a team that is responsible for student supervision, attendance, discipline, guidance, instructional leadership improvement, and a variety of student body activities. Previously, Dr. Kerns was an administrator at Dorman High School Freshman Campus in Spartanburg District Six.

After a successful career in business and restaurant management, Claretta now coaches, teaches and advises her staff and students on how to advance their careers and maximize their contributions to society.

Dr. Kerns received her B.A. in Business Administration from Loyola Marymount University in Los Angeles, CA, a B.A. in Education from Lesley University, Cambridge, MA, a degree in Educational Administration, and a Ph.D. in Education from South Carolina State University.

Dr. Kerns generously shares her time, talents, and resources serving the community through several Christian and church-affiliated organizations. She is a member of Golden Key International Honor Society, Computer Science Teachers Association, Delta Kappa Gamma Society International, and the South Carolina State Council of the International Reading Association. A big believer in giving back to her community, Kerns is a member of several organizations dedicated to supporting Christian organizations serving her local community.

Dr. Kerns is a highly-respected educator and mentor who has cultivated strong and valued relationships with parents and youth throughout Spartanburg County. She has a love for and dedication to the education of children. Her passion for helping uplift those who would be otherwise overlooked in the educational system can only be matched by the love that she has for her family and Christ.

Claretta and her husband, Odell, reside in Duncan, SC. They have four children and seven grandchildren and are active members of Church at the Mill in Moore, SC.

Mrs. Lottie Tolbert

(Photo courtesy of Mrs. Gloria Bridges)

"I loved spending time with Mom because she was always upbeat."

— Gloria Hinton Bridges

Mrs. Lottie Mae Eiland Tolbert

Written by Gloria Tolbert Hinton Bridges / Daughter

Thinking of my mom brings a serene smile to my face. She was the epitome of a mom! Lottie Mae Eiland was born in Louisville, MS in 1912. She was the oldest of four siblings. She never talked much about her childhood, but we knew she grew up on a farm, worked very hard, and didn't get to finish high school. Her birth mother died at an early age, and she had to help her father raise the younger children. Eventually, her father married a woman called Sarah. We all called her "Cousin Sarah." I never knew exactly why, but my mother did not like her and never thought of her as a mother. I think this experience made her want to be a great mom. I believe that she probably did the opposite of what she saw Cousin Sarah do.

In the mid-1920s, my mother met my father, Jesse S. Tolbert, in Macon, MS. He was a well-respected man in the community and had a great family. They fell in love and married. My grandfather owned a sawmill and the Whites in the community were out to get it. Realizing that he would not be able to tolerate conditions in the South much longer, he moved North to Detroit, MI where he was able to get a good job in the automobile industry. My father was the first in his family to make the "big move" North.

Once they were settled in Detroit, my mom immediately began to look for a job. She applied for a position as an elevator operator at J.L. Hudson's Department Store but did not get the job. Even in the North at that time, it would have been unusual for a Black woman to get that kind of job. She ended up doing what many Black women did back then, "day work" (cleaning houses). Because she was hard working with an independent personality, she thrived in Michigan. Although the job wasn't prestigious, it served her well. She had the flexibility and stability that she needed to raise her children. Looking back, I realize that she always thought working was very important for men and women. My mother became the Detroit connection for her family, and everyone stayed with us when they first moved to Detroit.

My parents had five children, of which I am the youngest. She instilled in all of us a sense of pride and responsibility, and the importance of getting an education. We were made to feel that we were special and therefore required to be the best person that we could be. Even though my father worked on the assembly line at Ford Motor Company, we had a middle-class mindset. When he was very young, Mom started telling my oldest brother he would become a doctor, and he did. She went back to high school herself at night and got a high school diploma. My parents wanted all of us to go to college, but my brother and I were the only two who achieved that goal.

Over the years, Mom became very active in New Light Baptist Church. My father became a deacon, and she became a deaconess. She was a natural leader and, eventually became president of one of the biggest organizations in our church. That organization spearheaded many activities and raised a great deal of money. I believe that my mom could have successfully led a large organization because she had a way with people. She was very energetic, kind, and loving. As president of the church women's organization, she was always busy planning meetings and activities. She remained president until she retired.

Because of the way she had grown up, she knew she had to have control over her family, however she also wanted her kids to enjoy themselves. She made sure that we were engaged in a lot of activities and stayed busy. Even though she did not have the example of her birth mother, she had an innate instinct about how to be a good mother. She had a good sense of humor and we all enjoyed and benefitted from her joviality. We learned to do housework and always had weekend chores. She was careful not to make us feel like servants, however, she also wanted us to have a sense of responsibility for our family life. Mom was also a great cook and loved to have people over for dinner. She loved seeing people enjoy one another and her food. We watched and learned the basics, but never took over. She did all the cooking. Despite this, we probably did less than most kids. We have a family joke about getting things done, we just call it "the Lottie Tolbert way."

Observing the way Mom handled her family and friends had a great impact on me. I feel that I am similar in many ways, and I am proud of it. I love people, have a good sense of humor, and raised my children to have a sense of responsibility and appreciation for higher education. I was easy-going in raising them and they both have easy-going personalities.

My mother always maintained contact with her relatives in Detroit and Chicago. Every year, we traveled either to Mississippi or Idlewild, MI, a Black resort in Michigan. Mom would cook and clean for everyone and at night the adults would play cards or go to various entertainment venues. We loved it! We were able to go swimming, skating, or just hang out together. I didn't realize how hard Mom worked "on vacation" until I was much older.

Gloria Bridges and her mother, Mrs. Lottie Tolbert
(Photo courtesy of Gloria Bridges)

As my siblings got married and moved out, I had more alone time with my mother. I went to college in Detroit, so I lived at home until I graduated. I loved spending time with Mom because she was always upbeat. When I moved to Atlanta with my husband, she was happy to come and visit and I was happy to have her with me. She was very proud that we had made friends and built a house there.

For some reason, my mother had a great desire to travel. She and my father went to California, New York, Hawaii, Italy, and many other countries. Because of my parents, we always had a worldview and knew there was a lot to see around the world.

Mom's club sponsored many bus trips to various places in Michigan. When I think about it, I am amazed that she knew as much as she did about the world. I think she inspired us and many others to love life and people and family. Everyone loved "Aunt Lottie," especially her husband and her children.

Gloria Hinton Bridges
West Bloomfield, MI

Mrs. Gloria Bridges
(Photo courtesy of Gloria Bridges)

Mrs. Gloria A. Bridges lives in Detroit, MI. She graduated from Wayne State University with a bachelor's degree in medical technology. She had a forty-year career in the medical technology field including tenures at Detroit Receiving Hospital and Providence Hospital, spending most of those years as a supervisor. In the early '70s, she established the lab and hired staff for the start-up, Detroit Medical and Surgical Center. In 1984 she secured a position at Herman Keifer, the Detroit Health Department, as principal medical technologist. She retired from there in 2006.

Gloria moved to Atlanta, GA with her husband and two children in 1979 to explore new social and employment opportunities. She met people from a variety of professions who were deeply involved in numerous social, civic, and political activities. This led her to become more involved also. She remained involved in Jack and Jill of America and later, Associates of Jack and Jill when she returned to Detroit in 1984. Gloria still gathers frequently with her lifelong Atlanta friends for social, family, and life events even though they are now scattered across the country.

Gloria is involved in her church, St. Stephen A.M.E., where she serves as President of the Scholarship Committee which focuses on helping young people acquire college scholarships. She is also involved in local civic and political activities. Gloria finds joy in encouraging and supporting her large family of children, grandchildren, siblings, nieces, and nephews. She is the recent widow of Dr. Nathaniel Bridges.

Mrs. Gloria Bridges

(Photo courtesy of Dr. Ayana Kilili)

"One of the greatest lessons that I have learned from my mom is to be strong, but not to be a martyr."

— Ayana Hinton Kilili, Ph.D.

HONORING

Mrs. Gloria Hinton Bridges

Written by Ayana Hinton Kilili, Ph.D. / Daughter

My mother, Gloria Hinton Bridges, is the youngest of five and was born several years after her parents moved from Mississippi to Detroit. She is beautiful, outgoing, smart, and a lot of fun. As a young person, she was active in church, often giving speeches and performing in plays. She graduated from Cass Technical High School which then, as now, was the most academically challenging high school in Detroit. When she grew up, it was rare for Black women to have college degrees in health-related fields, but she went to Wayne State University and graduated as a medical technologist. She worked in that career for over forty years. My mother has done so many things and she made it all look easy.

All my life, I have been told I look like my mother. I wasn't always so sure, but one day at my grandmother's house I found a black and white photo of a girl around twelve years old who looked a lot like me but, of course, could not have been me. It was a picture of my mother, and our resemblance was confirmed for me. As I grew into adulthood, the resemblances increased. I now know that I sound like my mom, I talk like my mom, and I laugh like my mom. To be told that I look like my mom is a compliment! She is a very beautiful woman. As I've grown, I realize that being told I am like my mother means so much more than having similar physical attributes, it is a much deeper compliment that also speaks to character.

One of the greatest lessons that I have learned from my mom is to be strong, but not to be a martyr. My mother worked hard in her career, rarely taking off and taking her responsibilities as a worker or supervisor seriously. She taught me that if you are going to do a job, you should do it well. However, she also showed me that there was no reason to work myself into the ground. She modeled for me that it is not only okay but also important to relax and recharge. Talking to my Black girlfriends, I've realized how rare is to be able to do both, work hard and practice self-care.

Mom was strong for my brother and me when we were young. Because she didn't want to burden us, she never let us know how hard things became at times. Although her family didn't always have a lot, she had a happy childhood. That was important to her, and she did her best to ensure that we had a happy childhood too. She experienced serious financial hardships and marital problems while my brother and I remained blissfully ignorant of most of it.

Gloria Bridges in Kenya
(Photo by Dr. Ayana Kilili)

My mother also taught me how important it is to be organized and have an orderly life. "A place for everything and everything in its place" was a mantra I learned from her. However, she also showed me that flexibility was better than rigidity. Sometimes it is necessary to "roll with the punches" rather than adhere to self-imposed restrictions. My mother gave me so much love and set boundaries and limits in my childhood that came from love. I didn't like that when I was sixteen instead of giving me a set curfew, she would calculate how much time it should take for me to get a meal and see a movie, and base my curfew on that specific outing but, I loved that she cared.

My mother taught me the importance of family. However, it wasn't a lesson that she repeatedly reinforced, it was something that she modeled. She expresses her love for her family (sisters, brothers, nieces, nephews, and others) in so many ways and they all love her in return. That strong family love began with the bond she had with her parents. When I was young, we moved to Atlanta, but we returned home to Detroit almost every Christmas because it was important to my mom to spend the holidays with her family. When my Grandma Lottie got too old to host the annual Christmas breakfast, my mother took over and has continued a tradition that must be around seventy years old now.

I remember how she cared for her mother-in-law, my Grandma Helen, when she was sick. Mothers and daughters-in-law are often shown on television as being at odds, but my mom and grandma's relationship was special. It was ultimately displayed in how my mother took care of Grandma Helen at the end of her life. Mom has taken care of her mother, brothers, and sisters, and has never complained or made her care for them about her. Taking care of one another is just a part of being a family.

My mother also modeled for me the importance of having good friends. Good friends are the extension of your family. They are the family of your choosing. They bring so much to your life and your children's lives. My mom has special lifelong friends whom she still travels to visit. She has a special group of friends from her days living in Atlanta that she sees regularly even though they are now scattered around the country. Mom has illustrated to me that it is critical to have good girlfriends that you can lean on when you need support and party with when you need to celebrate and have fun.

Mom is a great mother and, as a young mom, I'm trying to follow her example. Every day, as I find myself saying things to my kids that she said to me or doing things she did, I understand better the gift of herself that she has given me. I am my own person, but the values Mom gave me are my bedrock. They underpin everything that I try to accomplish at home and work. I'm not my mother's best friend and she's not my best friend. We're something deeper than that – I am my mother's daughter.

Ayana Hinton Kilili, Ph.D.
Pickerington, OH

Dr. Ayana Kilili
(Photo courtesy of Ayana Kilili)

Ayana Hinton Kilili, Ph.D. was born in Detroit, MI. Her family moved to Atlanta, GA for five formative years when she was in elementary school, but eventually, they moved back to Detroit, MI. She graduated from Cass Technical High School in 1991 and attended the University of Michigan where she earned a B.S.E in Chemical Engineering. She worked as an engineer for a few years before deciding to go to graduate school to work towards a Ph.D. at Wayne State University. She earned a Ph.D. in biochemistry and molecular biology in 2004 and moved to Boston, MA to work in a research lab at Tufts University.

Dr. Hinton met Dr. Geoffrey Kimiti Kilili at Tufts and they married in 2008. They moved to central Ohio when Ayana assumed a position as Assistant Professor in the biology department at Denison University where she has since earned tenure. On the path to earning tenure, she had two beautiful children, Atiya Kavinya and Kimiti Ukumyo Kilili. Ayana is currently serving as Associate Provost for Diversity, Equity & Inclusion and Director of Denison Forward, the college's diversity strategic plan. In her free time, Ayana has fun hanging out with her children and spending time with friends in the area. She also enjoys visiting family and friends in Detroit, throughout the US, and Kenya, her husband's homeland.

Afterword

Unfortunately, this anthology could not capture all the stories and relationships that my amazing female friends and family have with their mothers. However, I hope that it will inspire them to tell and write their stories. In this age when others are trying to interpret and write our history to suit their purposes, it is vitally important that we tell our own stories. Our children should know the strong shoulders on which they stand. They should be inspired and emboldened by their personal heritages of faith, service, wisdom, courage, and love.

I share this quote from Cicely Tyson's memoir, *Just As I Am* because it summarizes my prayer and hope for African American girls and women. I pray that we will continue to honor and bless ourselves, our mothers, and other Black women as we use our time and talents to serve others and fulfill God's will in our lives.

Ms. Tyson, I couldn't have said it better! Thank you!

From Just as I Am: A Memoir

By Cicely Tyson

"Make no mistake, my dear children: whether or not we recognize it, you and I were born into a legacy of trauma, just as surely as we've inherited our fore-parents' resilience . . .

No amount of Black girl magic, no repeated proclamations of our worth can fully treat the wound — although acknowledging its persistence is a beginning. The ultimate remedy, as I see it is supernatural. I look daily toward heaven for restoration, for spiritual healing. My true identity isn't rooted in our history, grievous and glorious as it is. It is grounded in my designation as a Child of God, the Daughter of the Great Physician. In His care, I find my cure.

My hope for you is the same one I carry for myself. I pray that amid the heartache of our ancestry, you can grant yourself the grace so seldom extended to us. I pray that you can pass that compassion on to your children and to their children so that it slathers comfort on our sore spots. I pray that, as a people, we can give ourselves a soft place to land. I pray even as we rightly express our fury as being regarded as sub-human, that we don't dwell in that space. That we don't allow anger to poison our spirits. That we embrace love as our One True Antidote. I hope, too, that you recognize your specialness, the distinctiveness the Creator has imbued us with. I see you as clearly as history has, and in unison with it, I nod. I know that swivel in your hips, that fervor in your testimony, that ebullience in your stride, that flair in your song. The fact that others are constantly trying to diminish you, ever attempting to dismiss your talents even as they mimic you, is proof of your uniqueness! No one bothers to undermine you unless they recognize your brilliance.

More than anything, I pray that you can carve out a purpose for yourself, a calling beyond your own survival, a sweet offering to the world. You gain a life by giving yours away. Not everyone is meant to raise a picket sign, and yet each of us can choose a path of impact. Rearing your children with affection and warmth is a form of activism. Honoring your word impeccably is a way to raise your voice.

Performing your job with excellence, with your chin high and your standards higher is as powerful as any protest march. Sowing into the lives of young people is a worthy crusade. That is what it means to leave this world of ours more lit up than we found it. It's also what it means to lead a magnificent life, even if an unlikely one."[1]

[1] Tyson, Cicely. *Just as I am*, pages 397 and 398-399. HarperCollins Publishers; New York, NY 10007

About the Author

Paulette Norvel Lewis is a retired workforce and career development specialist. She has been inspired and motivated by her work for historic civil rights leaders, Dr. Dorothy Height (as Interim Executive Vice President of the National Council of Negro Women) and Mrs. Coretta Scott King (as Chief of Staff). She has worked in several positions to place women of color in management positions in private industry, to facilitate their career advancement, and to advocate for equal pay and job equity for all women.

Paulette has always been inspired by the strength, resilience, creativity, courage, and brilliance of "Black Girl Magic" which led her to curate and compile this anthology, *My Mother's Daughter: A Heritage of Faith, Service, Wisdom, and Love.*

www.ingramcontent.com/pod-product-compliance
Lightning Source LLC
Chambersburg PA
CBHW041114120626
46547CB00019B/2710

9798990658929